Editorial

Eurasia in the World

The geopolitics of the Eurasian landmass are on the move. In this issue, we reprint the official foreign policy positions of China and Russia, which were published within days of each other in early spring 2023, when President Xi visited Moscow. Increasingly, China seems to be the senior partner in this relationship of states. This big change has unfolded gradually since the 1980s, when China and the Soviet Union began to move beyond their ideological rift. From 1979, Iran's departure from the western political camp reinforced the steady changes. Helena Cobban examines some of the practical consequences of these developments such as expanding rail networks and land-based supply routes.

Russia's war on Ukraine impacts Eurasia and geopolitical developments thereon. Russia made an historic mistake in invading Ukraine in February 2022. For more than two decades, Putin had patiently built constructive relations with the majority of the world's population. The BRICS formation brings together China and India, old foes, as well as strategic allies in South Africa and Brazil. Russia took the initiative in convening this forum, which musters considerable economic clout. The fifteenth BRICS summit will meet in South Africa later this year.

In September 2022, Indian Prime Minister Modi told Putin 'today's era is not an era of war'. At the same face-to-face gathering of the Shanghai Co-operation Organisation, Putin acknowledged China's 'questions and concerns' over Ukraine. So it is that Putin's illegal and deadly aggression against Ukraine has begun to undo his patient work of more than two decades to build alliances across and beyond the Eurasian landmass.

Back in 1997, Zbigniew Brzezinski saw the task confronting the United States thus:

> 'how America "manages" Eurasia is critical. Eurasia is the globe's largest continent and is geopolitically axial. A power that dominates Eurasia would control two of the world's three most advanced and economically productive regions...'

He summarised the task provocatively:

'The three grand imperatives of imperial geostrategy are to prevent collusion and maintain security dependence among the vassals, to keep tributaries pliant and protected, and to keep the barbarians from coming together.'

Brzezinski took a particular interest in Ukraine, describing it as an 'important space on the Eurasian chessboard'. He identified Ukraine, alongside Azerbaijan and Uzbekistan in Eurasia, as 'deserving America's strongest geopolitical support' — 'the critical state' among 'key Eurasian geopolitical pivots' due to its proximity to Russia.

So the war in Ukraine continues, with no end yet in sight. NATO remains the United States' 'chosen instrument of influence in Europe', as Frank Blackaby of SIPRI described it in 1996 (see *Spokesman 151*). Some 27 years later, this alliance against Russia continues to grow, with erstwhile neutral Finland now enrolled as a member and formerly neutral Sweden also impatient to come under the US nuclear umbrella. Meanwhile, a new generation of hydrogen bombs is apparently being shipped to US bases in Europe where they will be 'shared' with selected NATO allies. Extensive construction is under way at the recipient air bases, as well as Lakenheath near Cambridge in eastern England.

Putin's patience has seemingly run short in the face of these increasing military threats. Yet more forbearance and constructive engagement are urgently needed if escalation, possibly to nuclear exchanges, is to be avoided in and around Ukraine.

On 26 September 2022, three of the four Nordstream gas pipelines under the Baltic Sea, which run from Russia to Germany, were blown up. Counterintuitively at the time, it was put about that Russia was responsible. Why? It had no reason. Now Seymour Hersh has gone to press with how the US began planning to mine the pipelines before Russia invaded Ukraine in February 2022. The US government says Hersh's story is 'utterly false and complete fiction'. Nevertheless, the pipelines were destroyed and who benefited? Indeed, on 21 September 2022, Russia had mobilised military reservists having formally annexed four regions of Ukraine (Donetsk, Luhansk, Kherson and Zoporizhzhia).

What would Bertrand Russell make of current developments?

He would certainly be alarmed that Russia's war with Ukraine has been allowed to continue for a year without meaningful or effective attempts to bring about a lasting ceasefire. More positively, Russell would likely be supportive of the Treaty on the Prohibition of Nuclear Weapons which was eventually adopted at the United Nations in New York in 2017. It was the

The Spokesman

Eurasia in the World

Edited by Tony Simpson and Tom Unterrainer

Published by Spokesman for the Bertrand Russell Peace Foundation
Ken Coates: Editor 1970 to 2010

Spokesman 154   2023

CONTENTS

Editorial	3	Tony Simpson
Poem	6	Elena Shvarts
China's rise and the changing nature of global power	7	Helena Cobban
Global Security Initiative	23	PRC Ministry of Foreign Affairs
China's Position on Political Settlement of the Ukraine Crisis	34	PRC Ministry of Foreign Affairs
How Russia sees the World	37	Ministry of Foreign Affairs of the Russian Federation
Environmantal Injustice in Renewables	47	Dexter Whitfield
How John Ainslie influenced my life	57	Commander Robert Green
The Mistake	65	Claudia Delpero
Frightful Syllogism	71	Günther Anders
The Good Friday Agreement – 25 years on	82	Helen Jackson
Adult Education and Workers' Control	85	Tony Simpson
Workers' Control and Socialist Strategy	89	Tony Topham
Unions and Workers' Control	95	Colin Ward
What productivity?	98	Regan Scott
Poems	100	Elena Shvarts
Reviews	103	Barry Baldwin, Nigel Potter, Tom Unterrainer, Rae Street, Regan Scott, Stephen Winfield
Poem	122	Elena Shvarts

Cover: Freight train from China to Spain, inaugurated in 2014

ISSN 1367 7748   ISBN 978 0 85124 9254

Subscriptions
Institutions £40.00 (ex UK)
                    £33.00 (UK)
Individuals £20.00 (UK)
                    £25.00 (ex UK)

A CIP catalogue record for this book is available from the British Library

Published by
The Bertrand Russell Peace Foundation Ltd,
5 Churchill Park,
Nottingham, NG4 2HF
England
Tel. 0115 9708318
email:
editor@russfound.org
www.spokesmanbooks.org
www.russfound.org

Editorial Board
John Daniels
Kate Fleet
Stuart Holland
Henry McCubbin
Abi Rhodes
Regan Scott

FSC
Mixed Sources
Product group from well-managed forests and other controlled sources

Cert no. SGS-COC-006541
www.fsc.org
© 1996 Forest Stewardship Council

April 2023, freight train sabotaged close to Russia's border with Ukraine

product of decades of work, mainly by neutral and non-aligned countries such as Austria, Ireland, Mexico and New Zealand, and organizations such as the International Red Cross, which highlighted the catastrophic and unmanageable impacts of the use of nuclear weapons. Brazil and South Africa, two non-nuclear members of the BRICS formation, are amongst the 95 signatories to the Treaty, as is Kazakhstan, which in its Article Two declaration under the Treaty highlights the relevance of the Semipalatinsk Treaty on a nuclear-weapons-free-zone in Central Asia. The Soviet Union conducted some 460 nuclear explosions at the Semipalatinsk test sites. The local Kazakh population has to live with the aftermath of radioactivity and environmental degradation. Compensation for these victims of nuclear testing comes within the compass of the TPNW.

In 2018, the Permanent Five members of the UN Security Council, China, France, Russia, United Kingdom, and United States, issued a joint statement about the Nuclear Non-Proliferation Treaty (NPT) and the Treaty on the Prohibition of Nuclear Weapons (TPNW). Concerning the latter, they said 'it will not result in the elimination of a single weapon'. This was a rare display of common purpose, regrettably with destructive intent.

Russell would have been familiar with such cant. He would surely have related more positively to the high hopes and aspirations of those who champion the prohibition of nuclear weapons, whilst remaining sceptical and clear-sighted about the prospects for persuading the nuclear-armed states to give up their means of threatening mass death.

Tony Simpson

Istanbul did not fall, nor did Constantinople,
But the Third Rome came crashing down,
On the bottom of seas, under an emerald crust
In its ruins, in its ashes we burn.
I shan't see the gulfs, that is now quite clear,
Why should I want them? Why should I want Rome?
The world's not enough for me, and it's not safe,
It's all collapsed, we shiver in the embers.
Why should I want the world? All I need
Is for the angels not to hear me
But to listen to me, and sob bitterly,
Beclouding their under-eyes with circles of blue.

Elena Shvarts *1996*
translated by Georgina Barker

China's rise and the changing nature of global power

Helena Cobban

Helena Cobban is a long-time international affairs analyst and former columnist for The Christian Science Monitor *and* Al-Hayat *(London). This article was originally published on Globalities.org*

In the United States, relations between China and "the West" are viewed as a transoceanic affair, with the Asia-Pacific region forming its main arena of cooperation or competition. Viewed from Europe or West Asia (the area formerly known as the Middle East), relations with China look different: in recent decades the many land routes that crisscross Eurasia in all directions have been growing fast in length, connectivity, and capacity.

This could mark a big historical turning-point – or rather, a return after a 600-year hiatus to the kind of world in which, in the late 13th century CE, Marco Polo and his uncle travelled overland to, and through, large portions of China.

In the intervening centuries, it was the lethal *naval power* of a handful of small West European states and their American offspring that came to dominate the destinies of all of humankind. Everywhere they sailed in 15th through 20th centuries, those European-originated naval empires crushed the power of the large land-based polities they encountered. The Aztecs, Incas, Mughals, Ottoman, Ming and Qing Chinese, and numerous other empires and local confederations were all wiped out.

So now, 600 years after Portugal's Prince Henry the Navigator first started to build his network of heavily armed trading posts along the coasts of Africa, it looks as if land empires and the ties that bind them are about to make a comeback.

Let's look at some recent news stories. The *New York Times* reported on the numerous European leaders who have been visiting, or are now about to visit, Beijing.[1] "European leaders," the story says, "have been making a beeline to Beijing, *weighing their strategy toward China just as the United States intensifies pressure to pick sides in the growing acrimony between the two superpowers.*" Or, from West Asia, there was the slightly earlier news of China's leaders pulling off the diplomatic coup of *brokering a rapprochement between former foes Iran and Saudi Arabia.*[2] That latter news story can handily be supplemented with a recent *Bloomberg* piece about China and Iran collaborating on upgrading a key rail corridor that connects Russia (and potentially, also other European countries) much more speedily with ports in the Indian Ocean than is currently doable.[3]

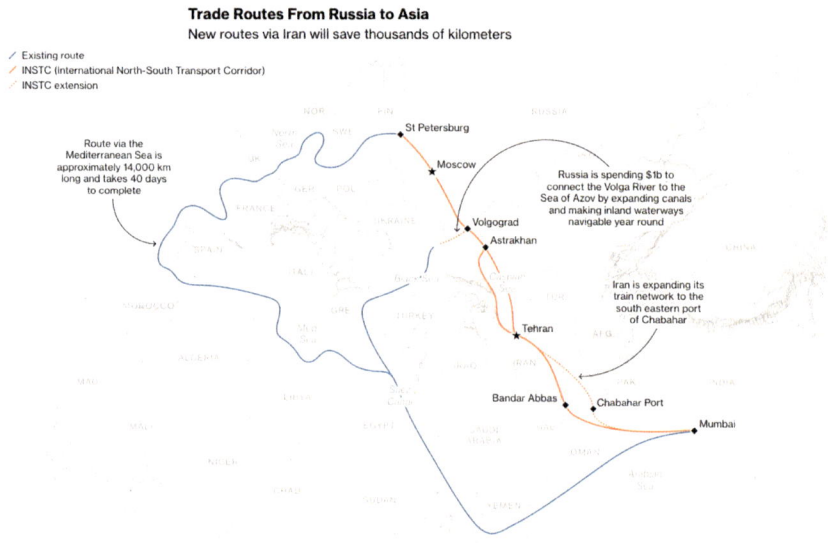

A quick digression by rail

Ever since the 19th century railroads have been – along with pipelines—a key ingredient of land power. They were key for the Anglo settlers along the US east coast who wanted to expand their colonies first across the Appalachians and soon after right across the continent. In the aftermath of WWII, they were key for the project of the visionaries who wanted to *end war in Western Europe by forming a European Union*. And more recently yet, they have been key in the push by China's leaders to spur growth in the whole of their large country while also integrating their economy with those of Central Asian nations and Russia (also known as the Belt and Road Initiative).

This map, from a 2016 *Financial Times* story[4] shows the Central Asian part of this growth – for pipelines as well as rail lines:

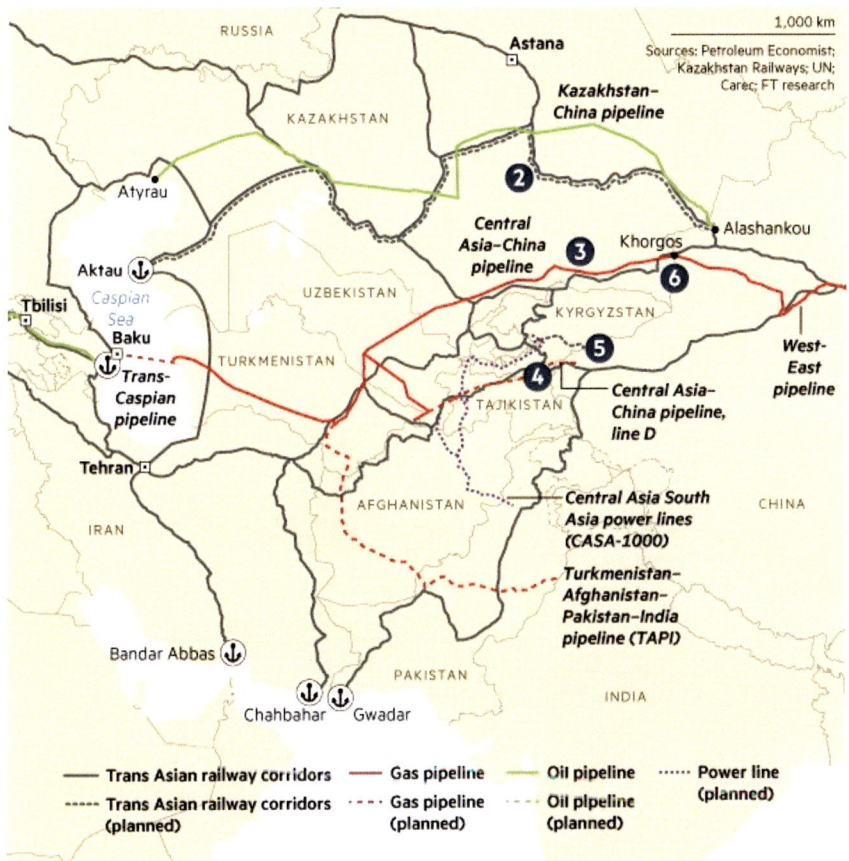

The following page shows a map (source: Wikipedia) of China's own *domestic high-speed rail lines* (CRH is short for China Rail Highspeed) together with a pie-chart indicating the usage of China's high-speed rail system compared with that of other countries. It's taken from the 2022 edition of an produced by the *Union International des Chemins de fer.*[5] The chart shows that China Rail (CR) had *more than 75% of the whole world's passenger-kilometers of high-speed rail travel in 2021*, at 606.4 billion p-km! Even with some possible disparities due to the pandemic, that is still astounding. France's SNCF came in a very distant second with 47.7 billion.

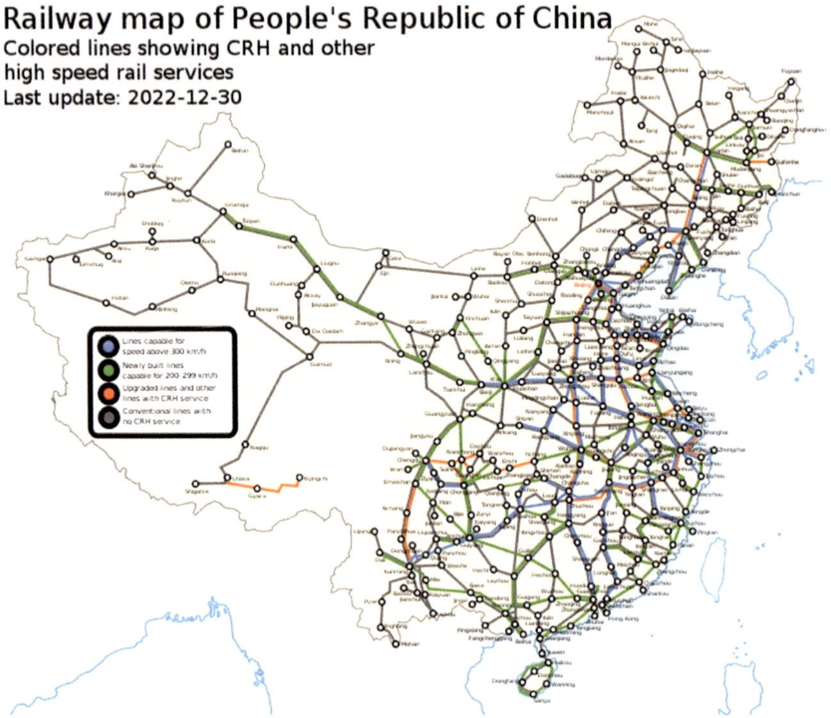

Railway map of People's Republic of China
Colored lines showing CRH and other high speed rail services
Last update: 2022-12-30

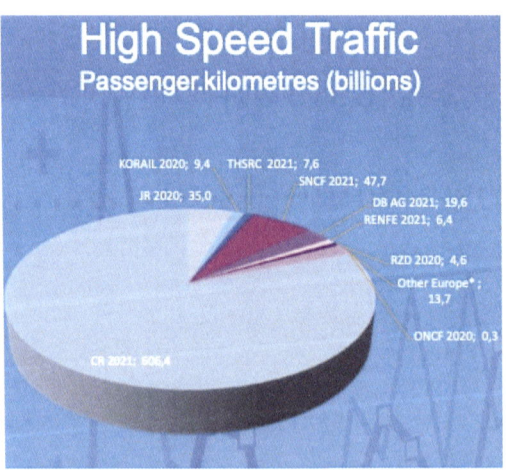

That same report has a plethora of other stats, too. I crunched some to come up with Table 1 about *total* p-kms travelled (not just the high-speed travelling) in various countries' rail systems. The figures are for 2021 again, except the USA (which barely had any, compared with the other entrants there.) Table 2 shows the usage of rail for *freight hauling* in these areas. From my work with the International Union of Railways (UIC) numbers, I draw these conclusions:

- China has been doing very well in building its domestic rail networks across the board – for moving both freight and passengers, and especially for passengers on the high-speed lines.

Country	Passenger-kms (mns)
India	1,050,738
China	946,499
Europe inc. Turkey	355,307
Russia	78,135
USA (AAR + Amtrak), 2020	3,593

▲ Table 1 Passengers

Figures for 2021, exc as noted	Freight tonne-kms (nms)	Surface area (1000s sq. kms)	1000s of tonne-kms per sq. km
Europe, inc. Turkey	3,026,339	10,964	276.0
Russia	2,544,800	17,098	148.8
China	2,404,200	9,563	251.4
USA, 2020	2,102,100	9,832	213.8
India	707,700	3,287	215.3

▲ Table 2 Freight

- Russia, which has a massive surface area, has used rail pretty effectively for hauling freight, but apparently less well for hauling people. (Note, though, that its population is only 10% of China's.)
- The USA is very far behind the rest of the developed world when it comes to passenger rail travel.

Parenthetically, as someone who has always loved rail travel, I have to admit that, now a denizen of Amtrak-land, I am *green with envy* as I learn more about rail travel in China and the plans for its further development. Ben Jones' very informative article[6] on China's high-speed rail system, from CNN (February 2022) says, *inter alia*, that:

No fewer than 37,900 kilometers (about 23,500 miles) of lines crisscross the country, linking all of its major mega-city clusters, and all have been completed since 2008.

Half of that total has been completed in the last five years alone, with a further 3,700 kilometers due to open in the coming months.

The network is expected to double in length again, to 70,000 kilometers, by 2035.

With maximum speeds of 350 kph (217 mph) on many lines, intercity travel has been transformed and the dominance of airlines has been broken on the busiest routes.

This last point is *extremely* important for the future of our planet. A 2019 report from the UK-based website Carbon Brief contains good stats on *how much more carbon-efficient rail travel is than flying or travelling in large cars.*[7] Here's one of their graphics:

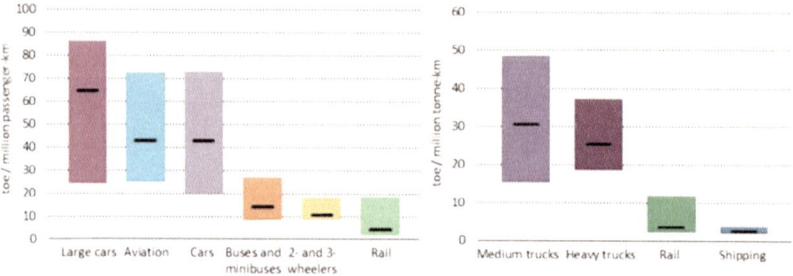

Energy intensity of different transport modes in 2017. The left-hand chart shows energy intensity of passenger transport, in tonnes of oil equivalent (toe) per million passenger km travelled. The right-hand chart shows energy intensity of freight transport, in toe per million tonne km transported. Source: IEA 2019.

Geopolitical implications

As I've indicated above, the deeply West-European-dominated power structure that has governed the world for the past few centuries was established and then maintained by maritime adventurers from a handful of small polities perched on the western (Atlantic) coast of Europe. These were, to take them chronologically by the date of the establishment of their empires, the following: 1. Portugal, 2. Spain, 3. England (later "Britain"), 4. Netherlands, 5. France.

I have written at length elsewhere about the origins, early history, and world-changing significance of Portugal's empire-building project,[8] and also about how those other four empires developed in the 16th and 17th centuries CE. The lessons I drew from those studies included the following:

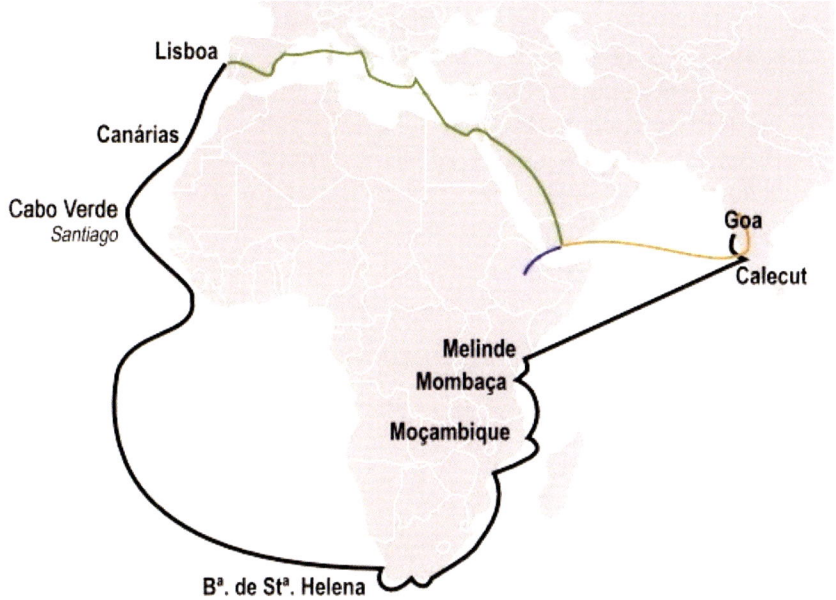

Da Gama's voyage to India (black.) Earlier Portuguese scouting parties took the other routes shown.

- When Portugal's Vasco Da Gama rounded the southern tip of Africa in 1498 and entered the already bustling maritime trade routes of the Indian Ocean, he brought with him levels of sustained cruelty and violence[9] that the peoples he found on and around this ocean had never seen before. That capacity for violence (both physically, in terms of the types of weapons available, and psychologically, in terms of the readiness to use them) underlay Portugal's ability to overpower many of the other polities they encountered – in India, the "Spice Islands" of East Asia, and elsewhere – and to lay the basis for the well-armed commercial empire they established in those places.
- The other four above-named polities then, over time, started competing with Portugal and each other to establish their (always well-armed) trading stations on all the world's continents. These deeply maritime empires all shared an ability to undertake, essentially, "hit and run" raids on the Indigenes they encountered which meant that even after enacting horrendous violence on these Indigenes, *they did not have to stay thereafter and live alongside them as neighbours...*[10] Then, after they'd established super-extractive plantations in some of those distant areas these Europeans had the ability (and the ever-present firepower) to (a) *work the local Indigenes to death on the plantations*, if they chose,

and then (b) replace those dead Indigenes as needed, with *labourers they had captured from elsewhere* in the empire and then transported across the ocean in conditions of chattel slavery.
- The birth and continuing development of these maritime empires itself helped in at least three of the cases – Portugal, Netherlands, England – to consolidate the emergence of a sense of "nationhood", including in linguistic and other cultural forms,[11] that otherwise would very likely not have existed or would have existed in a very different form.

It should not need to be noted here that in most cases, as convincingly demonstrated by Eric Williams and others, it was *the hyper-profits made from those processes of imperial extraction* that funded much of the "Industrial Revolution" in Europe.[12]

The unfolding of Anglo colonial rule in North America was slightly different from the above template, in two ways:

1. Here in Turtle Island, two centuries before Ian Smith tried to do the same thing in "Rhodesia", the expansionist extremists among the local settlers declared and successfully defended their "Unilateral Declaration of Independence" from their metropole in London.
2. For a century after 1776, the main focus of the United States' colonial-expansion practice was directed toward territorial expansion, not maritime expansion.

But the US Americans had brought with them from Europe a strong sense of cultural superiority over the Indigenes (whom they often saw as barely human), and the ability and willingness to use very lethal means to suppress them as they continued to steal their land and resources and to replace them with ever-new batches of settlers imported from Europe. Then, at the end of the 19th century, the final collapse of Spain's trans-oceanic empire in the Caribbean and East Asia gave the Americans a good chance to continue building their own maritime empire, in addition to the territorial one they had now finished conquering.

American missionaries, traders and naval vessels had anyway been plying the world's oceans since the early 19th century. In Japan, in 1853-54, Commodore Matthew Perry used the eight ships under his command to force the *shogun* in Japan to "open" up the country's ports to American traders. A decade before that, in July 1844, US naval power had already forced the Treaty of Wanghia onto the Qing empire of China.

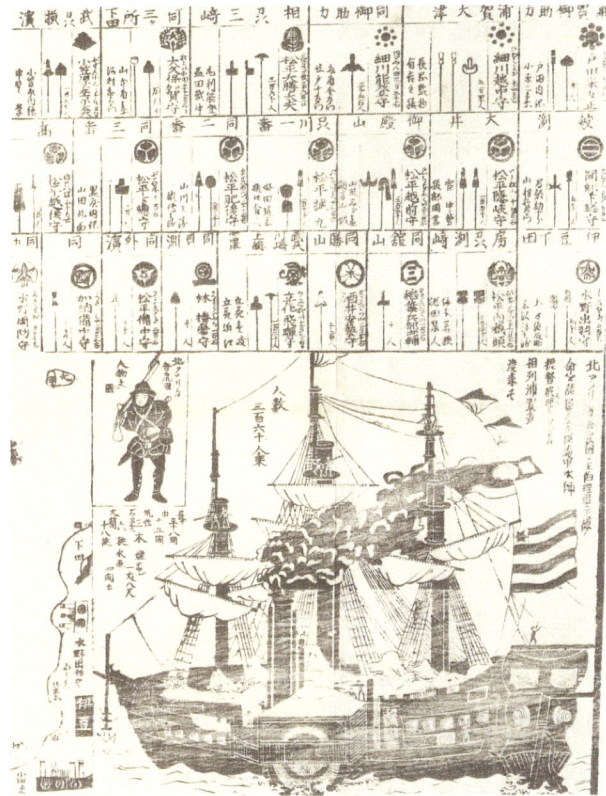

▲ Japanese woodblock print of Matthew Perry's small fleet

This treaty allowed the United States to establish largely self-governing outposts in Shanghai and four other Chinese cities, in which:

• American companies could conduct business on the same favoured terms that the British had earlier imposed on China in their just-concluded Treaty of Nanjing (which had guaranteed the British free access to China's huge market for *the opium that the British were very profitably cultivating in India*), and
• Chinese subjects would be tried and punished under Chinese law and American citizens would be tried and punished under the authority of the American consul or other public functionaries authorized to that effect.

At that point, the US government joined a whole string of West European governments – and Japan – in forcing upon China a series of

"Concessions" that significantly eroded China's sovereignty and freedom to determine its own destiny. Small wonder that most Chinese refer to the century that followed as "the century of humiliation." (Soon thereafter, at the other end of Asia, several West European powers came together to force a parallel series of Concessions on the rulers of the still-large, land-based, Ottoman Empire.)

▲ Schematic of the SIS and the French Settlement in Shanghai.

In Shanghai, to take one example of what ensued from the Chinese Concessions, in 1863 the British and American enclaves that had been allowed by the two treaties joined forces and created a largely self-governing enclave called the Shanghai International Settlement. (Unlike what happened in Hong Kong and Macau in that era, in the SIS the underlying sovereignty remained with China.) By 1905 the SIS had a population of 501,000. By 1925 this number had grown to 1.14 million. In 1941, the Japanese military occupied the whole of Shanghai including the SIS. In 1943, as part of the attempt by the USA and Britain to muster Chinese support against Japan, both governments agreed to return governance of the SIS and many of the other 19th-century "Concessions" areas to China. In 1949, the Chinese People's Liberation Army took over the whole of Shanghai during their victory over the Kuomintang.

The shifting nature of global power

For nearly the whole of the past 600 years, the power to transform and then to govern the international order has grown out of the barrel of a long-distance gun. For the first 500 of those years, the most influential of those guns were naval cannons; and then, over the course of the 20th century CE,

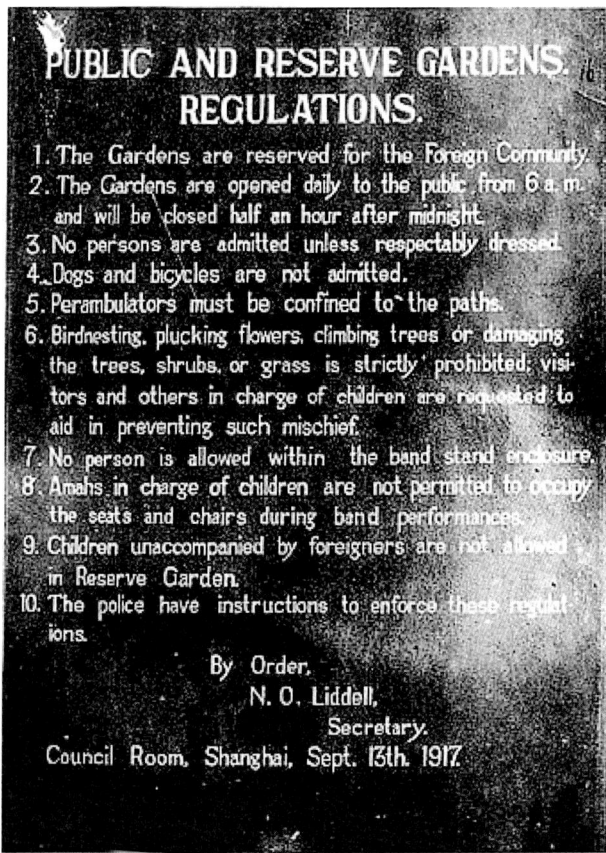

▲ 1917 notice in the SIS's main park

airpower came to also play a crucial role. Indeed, the United States' use of air-delivered nuclear bombs against Hiroshima and Nagasaki could be seen as the apotheosis of the long-distance bombardments that had since the beginning been a key marker of "Western" empires.

But the introduction of nuclear weapons into the global power balance then increasingly, over the years that followed 1945 (and especially after the Soviet Union's first nuclear weapons test in 1949), had the paradoxical effect of rendering not just their own use but also the use of increasing numbers and types of other long-distance/standoff weapons *increasingly unproductive and then, in political terms, actually counter-productive.*

In the 1950s, the North Koreans and their Chinese volunteer allies, who had no nuclear weapons and who were subjected to horrendous bombardments by the United States (including, quite possibly, by biological weapons) managed to fight the very powerful US intervention force in Korea to a standstill. In October 1962, after the United States and the Soviet Union came to the brink of the actual use of nuclear weapons during the Cuban Missile Crisis, *both sides backed down and agreed to a negotiated outcome.* In Vietnam, intense US bombing and other military actions were unable to stave off the victory of the North Vietnamese and their allies. Those same decades, intense military actions that Britain and France took against national liberation forces in imperial holdings in places like Malaysia, Aden, Algeria, or Kenya were similarly unable to prevent those forces from achieving their goal.

The demise of Portugal's longstanding empire in Africa was especially interesting. In 1974, discontent among the (mainly conscript) Portuguese forces fighting to suppress independence movements in Angola and Mozambique led those Portuguese units and their officers not just to give up the fight in Africa but also to *go home to Lisbon and overthrow the whole reactionary government there.*

The records of White South Africa and Israel – two European-origined settler-colonial outposts in the Global South – were also informative. In order to survive in the locations where they'd been planted, those outposts had to figure out a way to live alongside the various indigenous groups who were their neighbours and which they could not, in the world as organized after 1945, simply wipe out through genocide.

White South Africans fought a tough series of battles against local liberation forces until 1991, then finally agreed to a negotiated stand-down (on terms very favourable to themselves.) As for the Israelis, they demonstrated their considerable military might by using it against their neighbours repeatedly from 1947 and – in the case of Syria and Gaza – periodically until today. Throughout those decades, Israel's use of military force successfully forced Egypt and Jordan to sue for peace. But despite all the suffering Israeli violence has imposed on Palestinians since 1947, this violence has never succeeded in forcing Palestinians to give up their claims for full rights, including the rights to return and to self-determination.

Israel's use of force against Syria and Lebanon has proven similarly un- or counter-productive. The large-scale military assault that Israel launched against Lebanon in 1982 did succeed in forcing the Palestinian guerrilla units to leave Lebanon. But Israel's subsequent attempt to force a peace agreement on Lebanon itself proved short lived; and meantime the continuing presence of Israeli occupation forces in South Lebanon "succeeded" merely in incubating the new, militantly anti-Israeli Lebanese fighting force, Hezbollah. In 2006, an attempt by Israel to repeat its 1982 assault on Lebanon ended up a humiliating fiasco; and Hezbollah has remained deeply embedded in Lebanese society and politics ever since.

And then, in the current century, there have been Washington's massively sized – and budgeted – invasions of both Afghanistan and Iraq. We know how disastrous these two campaigns have been, at the humanitarian level, for the two countries' peoples (and their neighbours). But politically, what did they achieve for the United States? We must surely conclude that *the net political effect of each of them turned out to be extremely negative.*

In Afghanistan this is indubitable. The Taliban are back. The scenes of American allies fleeing for the exits in August 2021 left lasting marks worldwide. In Iraq, too, the net political effects for Washington have been very negative. The United States' lengthy occupation of Iraq fractured the whole country; incubated the Islamic State (IS); and sent waves of instability into Syria.

Meantime, the geopolitical impact of these two US military campaigns and the many other military or economic-punishment campaigns that Washington has waged in this century throughout the Global South – in Libya, Syria, Somalia, Venezuela, Mali, and elsewhere – has completely undercut the credibility of any claims the United States can make to being a power that "leads" or even just upholds the world political order.

China's longstanding campaign to grow its global political power has, by contrast, been built on very different foundations: primarily those of steadily strengthening economic ties with countries around the world while providing a strong example of how countries in the Global South can lift their people out of poverty and backwardness through sustained investment in infrastructure and economic development.

In the post-1945 world, it turns out, global political power no longer grows out of the mouth of a naval cannon or a "strategic" bomber, but rather from the thousands of kilometres of railroad track, the bridges and tunnels that carry their sleek passenger and freight trains, the towering cranes at fully automated ports, and the mouths of pipelines...

This is a wondrously welcome turn of events. Which is not to say that wars are no longer being fought (as we well know), or that force and violence have completely lost their role in world affairs. But if the past decades have shown us anything, it is that *campaigns to use massive military force at long distances from home are deeply counter-productive and that in most parts of today's global arena economic power and other forms of "soft" power have started to outperform the traditional tools of the military.*

The Ukraine-Russia paradox

Of course, I need to say something here about the ongoing conflict in Ukraine: a place where hard military power has clearly retained considerable importance.

My first observation is that the focus that the United States and its allies have placed for the past 20-25 years on long-distance/standoff weaponry in its campaigns in Afghanistan, Iraq, and elsewhere has left many of these Western countries very short of the basic materiél needed to wage large-scale ground warfare. And the steep decline that the broad manufacturing base in the United States and other NATO countries have seen over those same years makes it very hard just to speedily crank up military production lines in the way that was done in the 1940s or even the 1970s.

As US Joint Chiefs of Staff Chair Mark Milley and others have warned, there is a very real chance that within the coming weeks or months Ukraine's NATO backers will run out of the kinds of weaponry and ammo that the UAF's ground forces will needs if they are to hold their ground.

Another observation is that Washington's attempt to force Russia to its knees through the imposition of uber-punitive sanctions has not succeeded. Indeed, to the extent that its spurred many of the other members of "Team Sanctioned" and "Team Tarriffed" from around the world to collaborate on devising ways to reduce or end their exposure to such actions from Washington, the US sanctions on Moscow can be described as having been quite counter-productive.

In the Ukraine conflict, military force has not been shown to be un- or counter-productive. Far from it. But it is a certain kind of military force that is being used there: namely, large-scale ground forces on a scale not seen since WWII. And such forces, in those two countries as anywhere else, require a very robust manufacturing base to sustain them.

The return of China, land empires, and the Global South

On the surface of things, the three decades since the end of the US-Soviet Cold War seemed for a long time to be a period in which the United States exercised unchallenged hegemony over the international order. But underneath Washington's often arrogant flaunting of that power, changes of deep global significance were brewing. Those changes were at the level of both hard and soft power. Here's a quick initial list:

- The kinds of stand-off weapons that the US military gloried in developing and using were proving to have ever-lessening utility in effecting the stated real-world political goals.

- The arrogance with which Washington wielded those weapons, while bending many of the instruments of global governance to its will, provoked ever-growing resentment in the Global South. (The decision to invade Iraq in 2003 was a key turning point in this regard.)
- The hypocrisy with which Washington paraded itself as a supporter of "rights" while giving strong continuing support to Israel and other evident rights-abusers cost it dearly in terms of global soft power.
- The cruelty of the economic sanctions Washington maintained on countries like Iran, Cuba, Syria, and Venezuela further alienated millions of people throughout the Global South.
- The vigour with which US-dominated financial institutions like the World Bank and IMF worked to impose neoliberal policies on countries in the Global South imposed real hardships, especially when contrasted with the investments China was making in infrastructure development in many of these same countries.
- The selfishness with which Western countries guarded the patents to Covid vaccines, denying to pharma manufacturers around the world the ability to co-produce them ...

That list of US mis-steps and misapprehensions could go on and on. It's worth reiterating that the peoples of the Global South constitute a very strong majority of the whole of humanity, with the "White" countries of the "West" forming only around 12% of the whole. Also worth noting that most of the factors in any such list as that above are *factors of soft, not hard, power*.

The net result of all these processes has been the significant re-emergence onto the world scene of a China that is self-confident, smart, and strongly connected to other power centres across the Global South through ever-deepening economic ties and through a series of interlocking institutions like BRICS, the G20, the Shanghai Cooperation Organization, and the Asian Infrastructure Investment Bank.

In world-historical terms this is huge. It means that the 600-year era in which world affairs was dominated by self-righteous adventurers from a handful of small West-European countries, and their spawn, is now – finally – coming to an end.

Notes

1. Steven Erlanger and Matina Stevis-Grindneff, 'Even as US beckons, European leaders head to Beijing', *New York Times*, 29/03/2023

2. Helena Cobban, 'The China-Iran-Saudi handshake seen around the world', *Globalities*, 11/03/2023 (https://globalities.org/2023/03/the-china-iran-saudi-handshake-seen-around-the-world/)

3. Jonathan Tirone and Golnar Motevalli, 'Russia and Iran Are Building a Trade Route That Defies Sanctions', *Bloomberg*, 21/12/2022 (https://www.bloomberg.com/graphics/2022-russia-iran-trade-corridor/#xj4y7vzkg)

4. Jack Farchy and James Kynge, 'Connecting Central Asia', *Financial Times*, 09/05/2016 (https://www.ft.com/content/ee5cf40a-15e5-11e6-9d98-00386a18e39d)

5. International Union of Railways, 'Railisa UIC Statistics', 2022 edition

6. Ben Jones, 'Past, present and future: The evolution of China's high-speed rail network', 09/02/2022 (https://edition.cnn.com/travel/article/china-high-speed-rail-cmd/index.html)

7. Jocelyn Timperley, 'Eight charts show how 'aggressive' railway expansion could cut emissions', *Carbon Brief*, 30/01/2019 (https://www.carbonbrief.org/eight-charts-show-how-aggressive-railway-expansion-could-cut-emissions/)

8. Helena Cobban, 'Portugal and the origins of "the west"', *Project 500 Years*, 30/08/2021 (https://medium.com/project-500-years/portugal-and-the-origins-of-the-west-dd24fe8e2b4b)

9. Helena Cobban, 'More on Portugal's use of exemplary terror', *Project 500 Years*, 06/09/2021 (https://medium.com/project-500-years/more-on-portugals-use-of-exemplary-terror-742670dee0e1)

10. Helena Cobban 'The hubris of the long-distance empire', *Project 500 Years*, 19/08/2021 (https://medium.com/project-500-years/the-hubris-of-the-long-distance-empire-1158e174cf72)

11. Helena Cobban, 'Language, empire, nation, state', *Project 500 Years*, 13/09/2021 (https://medium.com/project-500-years/language-empire-nation-state-d9545c3fdc6f)

12. Eric Williams, *Capitalism and Slavery*, first published in the US in 1944 and most recently published as a Penguin Modern Classic (2022)

Global Security Initiative

Ministry of Foreign Affairs of the People's Republic of China

Published on 21 February 2023.

The Global Security Initiative Concept Paper

I. Background

The issue of security bears on the well-being of people of all countries, the lofty cause of world peace and development, and the future of humanity.

Today, our world, our times and history are changing in ways like never before, and the international community is confronted with multiple risks and challenges rarely seen before. Regional security hotspots keep flaring up, local conflicts and turbulence occur frequently, the COVID-19 pandemic persists, unilateralism and protectionism have risen significantly, and traditional and non-traditional security threats are entwined. The deficits in peace, development, security and governance are growing, and the world is once again at a crossroads in history.

This is an era rife with challenges. It is also one brimming with hope. We are convinced that the historical trends of peace, development and win-win cooperation are unstoppable. Upholding world peace and security and promoting global development and prosperity should be the common pursuit of all countries. Chinese President Xi Jinping has proposed the Global Security Initiative (GSI), calling on countries to adapt to the profoundly changing international landscape in the spirit of solidarity, and address the complex and intertwined security challenges with a win-win mindset. The GSI aims to eliminate the root causes of international conflicts, improve global security governance, encourage joint international efforts to bring more stability and certainty to a volatile and changing era, and promote durable peace and development in the world.

II. Core concepts and principles

1. Stay committed to the vision of common, comprehensive, cooperative and sustainable security. In 2014, President Xi Jinping initiated a new vision for common, comprehensive, cooperative and sustainable security, which has been widely recognized and supported by the international community. The essence of this new vision of security is to advocate a concept of common security, respecting and safeguarding the security of every country; a holistic approach, maintaining security in both traditional and non-traditional domains and enhancing security governance in a coordinated way; a commitment to cooperation, bringing about security through political dialogue and peaceful negotiation; and pursuit of sustainable security, resolving conflicts through development and eliminating the breeding ground for insecurity. We believe security will only be firmly established and sustainable when it is underpinned by morality, justice and the right ideas.

2. Stay committed to respecting the sovereignty and territorial integrity of all countries. Sovereign equality and non-interference in internal affairs are basic principles of international law and the most fundamental norms governing contemporary international relations. We believe all countries, big or small, strong or weak, rich or poor, are equal members of the international community. Their internal affairs brook no external interference, their sovereignty and dignity must be respected, and their right to independently choose social systems and development paths must be upheld. Sovereign independence and equality must be upheld, and efforts should be made for all countries to enjoy equality in terms of rights, rules and opportunities.

3. Stay committed to abiding by the purposes and principles of the UN Charter. The purposes and principles of the UN Charter embody the deep reflection by people around the world on the bitter lessons of the two world wars. They are humanity's institutional design for collective security and lasting peace. The various confrontations and injustices in the world today did not occur because the purposes and principles of the UN Charter are outdated, but because they are not effectively maintained and implemented. We call on all countries to practise true multilateralism; firmly uphold the international system with the UN at its core, the international order underpinned by international law and the basic norms of international relations underpinned by the UN Charter; and uphold the authority of the UN and its status as the main platform for global security governance. The Cold War mentality, unilateralism, bloc confrontation and hegemonism contradict the spirit of the UN Charter and must be resisted and rejected.

4. Stay committed to taking the legitimate security concerns of all countries seriously. Humanity is an indivisible security community. Security of one country should not come at the expense of that of others. We believe all countries are equal in terms of security interests. The legitimate and reasonable security concerns of all countries should be taken seriously and addressed properly, not persistently ignored or systemically challenged. Any country, while pursuing its own security, should take into account the reasonable security concerns of others. We uphold the principle of indivisible security, advocating the indivisibility between individual security and common security, between traditional security and non-traditional security, between security rights and security obligations, and between security and development. There should be a balanced, effective and sustainable security architecture, so as to realize universal security and common security.

5. Stay committed to peacefully resolving differences and disputes between countries through dialogue and consultation. War and sanctions are no fundamental solution to disputes; only dialogue and consultation are effective in resolving differences. We call on countries to strengthen strategic communication, enhance mutual security confidence, diffuse tensions, manage differences and eliminate the root causes of crises. Major countries must uphold justice, fulfil their due responsibilities, support consultation on an equal footing, and facilitate talks for peace, play good offices and mediate in light of the needs and will of the countries concerned. The international community should support all efforts conducive to the peaceful settlement of crises, and encourage conflicting parties to build trust, settle disputes and promote security through dialogue. Abusing unilateral sanctions and long-arm jurisdiction does not solve a problem, but only creates more difficulties and complications.

6. Stay committed to maintaining security in both traditional and non-traditional domains. In today's world, both the intension and extension of security are broadening. Security is more interconnected, transnational and diverse. Traditional and non-traditional security threats have become intertwined. We encourage all countries to practise the principles of extensive consultation, joint contribution and shared benefits in global governance, and work together to address regional disputes and global challenges such as terrorism, climate change, cybersecurity and biosecurity. There should be concerted efforts to explore multiple channels, develop a holistic solution, and improve relevant rules, so as to find sustainable solutions, promote global security governance and prevent and resolve security challenges.

These six commitments are interlinked and mutually reinforcing, and are an organic whole of dialectical unity. Among them, the vision of common, comprehensive, cooperative and sustainable security provides conceptual guidance; respecting the sovereignty and territorial integrity of all countries is the basic premise; abiding by the purposes and principles of the UN Charter is a primary benchmark; taking the legitimate security concerns of all countries seriously is an important principle, peacefully resolving differences and disputes between countries through dialogue and consultation is a must choice; and maintaining security in both traditional and non-traditional domains is an inherent requirement.

III. Priorities of cooperation

It is our common aspiration to achieve lasting world peace, so that all countries can enjoy a peaceful and stable external environment and their people can live a happy life with their rights fully guaranteed. Like passengers aboard the same ship, countries need to work in solidarity to foster a community of shared security for mankind and build a world that is free from fear and enjoys universal security.

To realize these visions, China is ready to conduct bilateral and multilateral security cooperation with all countries and international and regional organizations under the framework of the Global Security Initiative, and actively promote coordination of security concepts and convergence of interests. China calls on all parties to carry out single or multiple cooperation in aspects including but not limited to the following ones, so as to pursue mutual learning and complementarity and to jointly promote world peace and tranquility:

1. Actively participate in formulating a New Agenda for Peace and other proposals put forth in Our Common Agenda by the UN Secretary-General.

Support UN efforts to enhance conflict prevention and fully harness the peace-building architecture to assist post-conflict states in peace-building. Further leverage the Secretary-General's Peace and Security Sub-Fund of the China-UN Peace and Development Trust Fund and support a bigger UN role in global security affairs.

Support the UN in enhancing capacity for implementing its peacekeeping mandate, uphold the three principles of "consent of the parties, impartiality, and non-use of force except in self-defence and defence of the mandate" for peacekeeping operations, prioritize political solutions, and take a holistic approach to address both symptoms and root causes. Provide peacekeeping operations with adequate resources. Support the provision of sufficient, predictable and sustainable financial assistance to the African Union (AU) for it to carry out autonomous peacekeeping operations.

2. Promote coordination and sound interaction among major countries and build a major country relationship featuring peaceful coexistence, overall stability and balanced development. Major countries shoulder particularly important responsibilities of maintaining international peace and security. Call on major countries to lead by example in honouring equality, good faith, cooperation and the rule of law, and in complying with the UN Charter and international law. Adhere to mutual respect, peaceful coexistence and win-win cooperation, stick to the bottom line of no conflict and no confrontation, seek common ground while reserving differences, and manage differences.

3. Firmly uphold the consensus that "a nuclear war cannot be won and must never be fought". Comply with the joint statement on preventing nuclear war and avoiding arms races issued by leaders of the five nuclear-weapon states in January 2022. Strengthen dialogue and cooperation among nuclear-weapon states to reduce the risk of nuclear war. Safeguard the international nuclear non-proliferation regime based on the Treaty on the Non-proliferation of Nuclear Weapons (NPT) and actively support the efforts of countries in relevant regions to establish nuclear-weapon-free zones. Promote international cooperation on nuclear security, so as to build a fair, collaborative and mutually beneficial international nuclear security system.

4. Fully implement the resolution of Promoting International Cooperation on Peaceful Uses in the Context of International Security adopted by the

76th session of the UN General Assembly.

Carry out cooperation under such frameworks as the UN Security Council's 1540 Committee, the Chemical Weapons Convention (CWC) and the Biological Weapons Convention (BWC), promote complete prohibition and thorough destruction of weapons of mass destruction, and build up the capacity of all countries in areas including non-proliferation export control, biosecurity and protection against chemical weapons.

Support the process of global conventional arms control. Support cooperation among China, Africa and Europe on small arms and light weapons control under the premise of respecting the will of Africa. Support the implementation of the initiative of Silencing the Guns in Africa. Actively carry out international cooperation and assistance on humanitarian demining and provide help to affected countries as much as one's ability permits.

5. Promote political settlement of international and regional hotspot issues. Encourage the countries concerned to overcome differences and resolve hotspots through candid dialogue and communication. Support the international community in constructively participating in the political settlement of hotspots, under the premise of non-interference in internal affairs, mainly through the means of facilitating peace talks, with fairness and practicality as the main attitude, and mainly following the approach of addressing both symptoms and root causes. Support political settlement of hotspot issues such as the Ukraine crisis through dialogue and negotiation.

6. Support and improve the ASEAN-centered regional security cooperation mechanism and architecture, and adhere to the ASEAN way of consensus-building and accommodating each other's comfort level to further strengthen security dialogue and cooperation among regional countries. Support efforts to promote cooperation in non-traditional security areas under the framework of Lancang-Mekong Cooperation (LMC), implement relevant cooperation projects under the LMC Special Fund, and strive to foster a pilot zone for GSI to jointly safeguard regional peace and stability.

7. Implement the five-point proposal on realizing peace and stability in the Middle East, including advocating mutual respect, upholding equity and justice, realizing non-proliferation, jointly fostering collective security, and accelerating development cooperation, so as to jointly establish a new security framework in the Middle East. Support the positive momentum

and the efforts of Middle East countries to strengthen dialogue and improve their relations, accommodate the reasonable security concerns of all parties, strengthen the internal forces of safeguarding regional security, and support the League of Arab States (LAS) and other regional organizations in playing a constructive role in this regard. The international community should take practical steps to advance the two-state solution to the Palestinian question, and convene a larger, more authoritative and more influential international peace conference, so as to achieve a just solution to the Palestinian question at an early date.

8. Support the efforts of African countries, the AU and sub-regional organizations to resolve regional conflicts, fight terrorism and safeguard maritime security, call on the international community to provide financial and technical support to Africa-led counter-terrorism operations, and support African countries in strengthening their ability to safeguard peace independently. Support addressing African problems in the African way, and promote peaceful settlement of hotspots in the Horn of Africa, the Sahel, the Great Lakes region and other areas. Actively implement the Outlook on Peace and Development in the Horn of Africa, promote the institutionalization of the China-Horn of Africa Peace, Governance and Development Conference, and work actively to launch pilot projects of cooperation.

9. Support Latin American and Caribbean countries in actively fulfilling commitments stated in the *Proclamation of Latin America and the Caribbean as a Zone of Peace*, and support the Community of Latin American and Caribbean States and other regional and sub-regional organizations in playing an active role in upholding regional peace and security and properly handling regional hotspots.

10. Pay high attention to the special situation and legitimate concerns of Pacific island countries in regard to climate change, natural disasters and public health, support the efforts of Pacific island countries to address global challenges, and support island countries in implementing the 2050 Strategy for the Blue Pacific Continent. Increase the provision of materials, funds and talents to help island countries improve their ability to deal with non-traditional security threats.

11. Strengthen maritime dialogue and exchange and practical cooperation, properly handle maritime differences, and work together to tackle

transnational crimes at sea including piracy and armed robbery, so as to jointly safeguard maritime peace and tranquility and sea lane security. Call on upstream and downstream countries along trans-boundary rivers to actively engage in international cooperation, resolve relevant disputes through dialogue and consultation, ensure the safety of shipping on trans-boundary rivers, rationally utilize and protect water resources, and protect the ecological environment of trans-boundary rivers.

12. Strengthen the UN's role as the central coordinator in the global fight against terrorism, support the international community in fully implementing the UN General Assembly and Security Council counter-terrorism resolutions and the UN Global Counter-Terrorism Strategy, and jointly crack down on all terrorist organizations and individuals designated by the Security Council. Channel more global counter-terrorism resources to developing countries to enhance their counter-terrorism capacity building. Oppose linking terrorism with any particular country, ethnic group or religion. Enhance studies on and responses to the impact of emerging technologies on global counter-terrorism efforts.

13. Deepen international cooperation in the field of information security. China has put forward the *Global Initiative on Data Security* and calls for joint efforts to formulate global rules on digital governance that reflect the will and respect the interests of all parties. Follow through on the *China-LAS Cooperation Initiative on Data Security and the Data Security Cooperation Initiative of China+Central Asia*, jointly address various cyber threats, and work to establish a global governance system on cyberspace featuring openness and inclusion, justice and fairness, security and stability, vigour and vitality.

14. Strengthen biosecurity risk management. Jointly advocate responsible bioscience research and encourage all stakeholders to refer to the *Tianjin Biosecurity Guidelines for Codes of Conduct for Scientists* on a voluntary basis. Jointly strengthen the building of biosecurity capability of laboratories, reduce biosecurity risks and promote the healthy development of biotechnology.

15. Strengthen international security governance on artificial intelligence (AI) and other emerging technologies, and prevent and manage potential security risks. China has issued position papers on regulating military applications and strengthening ethical governance of AI, and stands ready

to strengthen communication and exchange with the international community on AI security governance, promote the establishment of an international mechanism with broad participation, and develop governance frameworks, standards and norms based on extensive consensus.

16. Strengthen international cooperation on outer space and safeguard the international order in outer space underpinned by international law. Carry out activities in outer space in accordance with international law, safeguard the safety of in-orbit astronauts and the long-term and sustainable operation of space facilities. Respect and ensure the equal right of all countries to use outer space peacefully. Resolutely reject the weaponization of and arms race in outer space, and support the negotiation and conclusion of an international legal instrument on arms control in outer space.

17. Support the World Health Organization in playing a leading role in global governance in public health, and effectively coordinate and mobilize global resources to jointly respond to COVID-19 and other major global infectious diseases.

18. Safeguard global food and energy security. Strengthen action coordination to maintain the smooth operation of international agricultural trade, ensure stable grain production and smooth supply chains, and avoid politicizing and weaponizing food security issues. Strengthen international energy policy coordination, create a safe and stable environment for ensuring energy transportation, and jointly maintain the stability of the global energy market and energy prices.

19. Fully and effectively implement the UN Convention against Transnational Organized Crime. Encourage all countries to conclude or join international treaties, conventions or agreements or make institutional arrangements to fight transnational crimes. Support the three international drug control conventions of the UN, safeguard the international drug control system, and advocate coordination, shared responsibility and sincere cooperation in the international community to jointly address challenges posed by the drug problem and build a community with a shared future for mankind that is free from the harm of drugs. Actively conduct law enforcement cooperation on the basis of respecting each country's sovereignty, so as to jointly improve law enforcement capacity and security governance. Support the establishment of a global training

system to train for developing countries more law enforcement officers who are responsive to their countries' security needs.

20. Support the cooperation among countries in addressing climate change and maintaining stable and smooth supply and industrial chains, and speed up the implementation of the UN 2030 Agenda for Sustainable Development in order to promote sustainable security through sustainable development.

IV. Platforms and mechanisms of cooperation

1. Engage in wide-ranging discussions and communication on peace and security at the General Assembly, relevant UN Committees, the Security Council, relevant institutions, and other international and regional organizations based on their respective mandates, and put forward common initiatives and propositions to forge consensus in the international community to address security challenges.

2. Leverage the roles of the Shanghai Cooperation Organization, BRICS cooperation, the Conference on Interaction and Confidence Building Measures in Asia, the "China+Central Asia" mechanism, and relevant mechanisms of East Asia cooperation, and carry out security cooperation incrementally to achieve similar or same goals. Promote the establishment of a multilateral dialogue platform in the Gulf region and give play to the role of coordinating and cooperative mechanisms such as the Meeting of Foreign Ministers of the Neighboring Countries of Afghanistan and the China-Horn of Africa Peace, Governance and Development Conference to promote regional and global peace and stability.

3. Hold high-level conferences on the GSI in due course to strengthen policy communication in the field of security, promote intergovernmental dialogue and cooperation, and further foster synergy in the international community to address security challenges.

4. Support the China-Africa Peace and Security Forum, the Middle East Security Forum, the Beijing Xiangshan Forum, the Global Public Security Cooperation Forum (Lianyungang) and other international dialogue platforms in contributing to deepening exchange and cooperation on security. Promote the establishment of more global security forums to provide new platforms for governments, international organizations, think tanks and social organizations to leverage their advantages and participate

in global security governance.

5. Build more international platforms and mechanisms for exchange and cooperation on addressing security challenges in such areas as counter-terrorism, cybersecurity, biosecurity and emerging technologies, with a view to improving the governance capacity in the domain of non-traditional security. Encourage more exchanges and cooperation among university-level military and police academies. China is willing to provide other developing countries with 5,000 training opportunities in the next five years to train professionals for addressing global security issues.

The GSI, following the principle of openness and inclusiveness, welcomes and looks forward to the participation of all parties to jointly enrich its substance and actively explore new forms and areas of cooperation. China stands ready to work with all countries and peoples who love peace and aspire to happiness to address all kinds of traditional and non-traditional security challenges, protect the peace and tranquility of the earth, and jointly create a better future for mankind, so that the torch of peace will be passed on from generation to generation and shine across the world.

Source: fmprc.gov.cn/eng/wjbxw/202302/t20230221_11028348.html

China's Position on Political Settlement of the Ukraine Crisis

Ministry of Foreign Affairs of the People's Republic of China

Published on 24 February 2023.

1. Respecting the sovereignty of all countries. Universally recognized international law, including the purposes and principles of the United Nations Charter, must be strictly observed. The sovereignty, independence and territorial integrity of all countries must be effectively upheld. All countries, big or small, strong or weak, rich or poor, are equal members of the international community. All parties should jointly uphold the basic norms governing international relations and defend international fairness and justice. Equal and uniform application of international law should be promoted, while double standards must be rejected.

2. Abandoning the Cold War mentality. The security of a country should not be pursued at the expense of others. The security of a region should not be achieved by strengthening or expanding military blocs. The legitimate security interests and concerns of all countries must be taken seriously and addressed properly. There is no simple solution to a complex issue. All parties should, following the vision of common, comprehensive, cooperative and sustainable security and bearing in mind the long-term peace and stability of the world, help forge a balanced, effective and sustainable European security architecture. All parties should oppose the pursuit of one's own security at the cost of others' security, prevent bloc confrontation, and work together for peace and stability on the Eurasian Continent.

3. Ceasing hostilities. Conflict and war benefit no one. All parties must stay rational and exercise restraint, avoid fanning the flames and aggravating tensions, and prevent the crisis from deteriorating further or even spiralling out of control. All parties should support Russia and Ukraine in working in the same direction and resuming direct dialogue as quickly as possible, so as to gradually deescalate the situation and ultimately reach a comprehensive ceasefire.

4. Resuming peace talks. Dialogue and negotiation are the only viable solution to the Ukraine crisis. All efforts conducive to the peaceful settlement of the crisis must be encouraged and supported. The international community should stay committed to the right approach of promoting talks for peace, help parties to the conflict open the door to a political settlement as soon as possible, and create conditions and platforms for the resumption of negotiation. China will continue to play a constructive role in this regard.

5. Resolving the humanitarian crisis. All measures conducive to easing the humanitarian crisis must be encouraged and supported. Humanitarian operations should follow the principles of neutrality and impartiality, and humanitarian issues should not be politicized. The safety of civilians must be effectively protected, and humanitarian corridors should be set up for the evacuation of civilians from conflict zones. Efforts are needed to increase humanitarian assistance to relevant areas, improve humanitarian conditions, and provide rapid, safe and unimpeded humanitarian access, with a view to preventing a humanitarian crisis on a larger scale. The UN should be supported in playing a coordinating role in channelling humanitarian aid to conflict zones.

6. Protecting civilians and prisoners of war (POWs). Parties to the conflict should strictly abide by international humanitarian law, avoid attacking civilians or civilian facilities, protect women, children and other victims of the conflict, and respect the basic rights of POWs. China supports the exchange of POWs between Russia and Ukraine, and calls on all parties to create more favourable conditions for this purpose.

7. Keeping nuclear power plants safe. China opposes armed attacks against nuclear power plants or other peaceful nuclear facilities, and calls on all parties to comply with international law including the Convention on Nuclear Safety (CNS) and resolutely avoid man-made nuclear accidents. China supports the International Atomic Energy Agency (IAEA) in playing a constructive role in promoting the safety and security of peaceful nuclear facilities.

8. Reducing strategic risks. Nuclear weapons must not be used and nuclear wars must not be fought. The threat or use of nuclear weapons should be opposed. Nuclear proliferation must be prevented and nuclear crisis avoided. China opposes the research, development and use of chemical and biological weapons by any country under any circumstances.

9. Facilitating grain exports. All parties need to implement the Black Sea Grain Initiative signed by Russia, Türkiye, Ukraine and the UN fully and effectively in a balanced manner, and support the UN in playing an important role in this regard. The cooperation initiative on global food security proposed by China provides a feasible solution to the global food crisis.

10. Stopping unilateral sanctions. Unilateral sanctions and maximum pressure cannot solve the issue; they only create new problems. China opposes unilateral sanctions unauthorized by the UN Security Council. Relevant countries should stop abusing unilateral sanctions and "long-arm jurisdiction" against other countries, so as to do their share in deescalating the Ukraine crisis and create conditions for developing countries to grow their economies and better the lives of their people.

11. Keeping industrial and supply chains stable. All parties should earnestly maintain the existing world economic system and oppose using the world economy as a tool or weapon for political purposes. Joint efforts are needed to mitigate the spillovers of the crisis and prevent it from disrupting international cooperation in energy, finance, food trade and transportation and undermining the global economic recovery.

12. Promoting post-conflict reconstruction. The international community needs to take measures to support post-conflict reconstruction in conflict zones. China stands ready to provide assistance and play a constructive role in this endeavour.

How Russia sees the World

Ministry of Foreign Affairs of the Russian Federation

Russia's revised Foreign Policy Concept was published on 31 March 2023. This excerpt is taken from the unofficial translation published on the website of the Ministry of Foreign Affairs of the Russian Federation. It spells out Russia's public position in relation to its neighbours around the world in rather less strident terms than many other public pronouncements by President Putin and Foreign Minister Lavrov. Ukraine is mentioned once elsewhere in the document:

'Considering the strengthening of Russia as one of the leading centres of development in the modern world and its independent foreign policy as a threat to Western hegemony, the United States of America (USA) and their satellites used the measures taken by the Russian Federation as regards Ukraine to protect its vital interests as a pretext to aggravate the longstanding anti-Russian policy and unleashed a new type of hybrid war.'

* * *

Regional tracks of the foreign policy of the Russian Federation

Near Abroad

49. The most important for the security, stability, territorial integrity and social and economic development of Russia, strengthening its position as one of the influential sovereign centres of world development and civilization is to ensure sustainable long-term good-neighbourly relations and to combine the strengths in various fields with the CIS

[Commonwealth of Independent States] member states, which are connected with Russia by centuries-old traditions of joint statehood, deep interdependence in various fields, a common language and close cultures. With the purpose of further transformation of the near abroad into a zone of peace, good neighbourliness, sustainable development and prosperity, the Russian Federation intends to give priority to:

1) preventing and resolving armed conflicts, improving inter-state relations, and ensuring stability in the near abroad, including preventing the instigation of 'colour revolutions' and other attempts to interfere in the internal affairs of Russia's allies and partners;

2) ensuring guaranteed protection of Russia, its allies and partners under any military and political scenario in the world, strengthening the system of regional security based on the principle of indivisibility of security and Russia's key role in maintaining and strengthening regional security, the complementarity of the Union State [with Belarus], the CSTO [Collective Security Treaty Organization] and other formats of interaction between Russia and its allies and partners in the defence and security sphere;

3) countering deployment or reinforcement of military infrastructure of unfriendly states and other threats to Russia's security in the near abroad;

4) deepening integration processes, which serve Russia's interests, and strategic cooperation with the Republic of Belarus, strengthening the mutually beneficial comprehensive cooperation system based on combined CIS and EAEU [Eurasian Economic Union] potentials, as well as developing additional multilateral formats, including a mechanism for interaction between Russia and the states of the Central Asian region;

5) establishing an integrated economic and political space in Eurasia in the long term;

6) preventing and countering unfriendly actions of foreign states and their alliances, which provoke disintegration processes in the near abroad and create obstacles to the exercise of the sovereign right of Russia's allies and partners to deepen their comprehensive cooperation with Russia;

7) unleashing the economic potential of good-neighbourliness, primarily with the EAEU member states and states interested in developing economic relations with Russia in order to form a broader integration contour in Eurasia;

8) comprehensively supporting the Republic of Abkhazia and the Republic of South Ossetia, promoting the voluntary choice, based on international law, of the peoples of these states in favour of a deeper integration with Russia;

9) strengthening cooperation in the Caspian Sea zone, proceeding from

the premise that the solution of all issues relating to this region falls within the exclusive competence of the five Caspian states.

The Arctic

50. Russia is seeking to preserve peace and stability, enhance environmental sustainability, reduce threats to national security in the Arctic, create favourable international conditions for the social and economic development of the Arctic zone of the Russian Federation (including to protect the original habitat and traditional livelihood of the indigenous people living there), as well as to advance the Northern Sea Route as a competitive national transport corridor making possible its international use for transportations between Europe and Asia. In pursuing these aims, the Russian Federation is going to focus on:

1) peacefully resolving international issues, related to the Arctic, proceeding from the premise of the special responsibility of the Arctic states for the sustainable development of the region and the sufficiency of the United Nations Convention on the Law of the Sea dated 10 December 1982 for regulating interstate relations in the Arctic Ocean (including protecting the marine environment and delimitating maritime areas);

2) counteracting the unfriendly states' policy aimed at militarization of the region and limiting Russia's ability to exercise its sovereign rights in the Arctic zone of the Russian Federation;

3) ensuring the unalterability of the historically established international legal regime of the inland maritime waters of the Russian Federation;

4) establishing a mutually beneficial cooperation with the non Arctic states pursuing a constructive policy toward Russia and interested in international activities in the Arctic, including developing infrastructure of the Northern Sea Route.

Eurasian continent
The People's Republic of China, the Republic of India

51. A comprehensive deepening of ties and enhancement of coordination with friendly sovereign global centres of power and development, which are located on the Eurasian continent and committed to approaches which coincide in principle with the Russian approaches to a future world order and solutions for key problems of the world politics, is particularly important for achieving strategic goals and major objectives of the foreign policy of the Russian Federation.

52. Russia aims at further strengthening the comprehensive partnership and the strategic cooperation with the People's Republic of China and

focuses on the development of a mutually beneficial cooperation in all areas, provision of mutual assistance, and enhancement of coordination in the international arena to ensure security, stability and sustainable development at the global and regional levels, both in Eurasia and in other parts of the world.

53. Russia will continue to build up a particularly privileged strategic partnership with the Republic of India with a view to enhance and expand cooperation in all areas on a mutually beneficial basis and place special emphasis on increasing the volume of bilateral trade, strengthening investment and technological ties, and ensuring their resistance to destructive actions of unfriendly states and their alliances.

54. Russia seeks to transform Eurasia into a continental common space of peace, stability, mutual trust, development and prosperity. Achieving this goal implies:

1) comprehensive strengthening of the SCO's [Shanghai Co-operation Organsation] potential and role in ensuring security in Eurasia and promoting its sustainable development by enhancing the Organization's activities in the light of current geopolitical realities;

2) establishment of the broad Greater Eurasian Partnership integration contour by combining the potential of all the states, regional organizations and Eurasian associations, based on the EAEU, the SCO and the Association of Southeast Asian Nations (ASEAN) as well as the conjunction of the EAEU development plans and the Chinese initiative 'One Belt One Road' while preserving the possibility for all the interested states and multilateral associations of the Eurasian continent to participate in this partnership and – as a result – establishment of a network of partner organizations in Eurasia;

3) strengthening of the economic and transport interconnectivity in Eurasia, including through the modernization and increased capacity of the Baikal-Amur Mainline and the Trans-Siberian railway; the rapid launch of the International North–South Transport Corridor; improvement of infrastructure of the Western Europe–Western China International Transit Corridor, the Caspian and the Black Sea regions, and the Northern Sea Route; creation of development zones and economic corridors in Eurasia, including the China–Mongolia–Russia economic corridor, as well as increased regional cooperation in digital development and establishment of an energy partnership.

4) comprehensive settlement in Afghanistan, assistance in building it as a sovereign, peaceful and neutral State with stable economy and political system which meets the interests of all the ethnic groups living there and

opens up prospects for integrating Afghanistan into the Eurasian space for cooperation.

The Asia-Pacific region

55. Given the dynamically growing multifaceted potential of the Asia-Pacific region, the Russian Federation is going to focus on:

1) increasing economic, security, humanitarian and other cooperation with the states of the region and the ASEAN member states;

2) establishing a comprehensive, open, indivisible, transparent, multilateral and equitable architecture of security and mutually beneficial cooperation in the region based on a collective and non-aligned approaches as well as unleashing the region's potential aiming at the establishment of a Great Eurasian Partnership;

3) promoting constructive non-politicized dialog and interstate cooperation in various areas, including with the help of opportunities provided by the Asia-Pacific Economic Cooperation forum;

4) countering attempts to undermine the regional system of multilateral security and development alliances on the basis of ASEAN, which rests upon the principles of consensus and equality of its participants;

5) developing a broad international cooperation to counter policies aimed at drawing dividing lines in the region.

The Islamic world

56. The states of friendly Islamic civilization, which has great prospects for establishing itself as an independent centre of world development within a polycentric world, are increasingly in demand and more reliable partners of Russia in ensuring security and stability as well as in solving economic problems at the global and regional levels. Russia seeks to strengthen the comprehensive mutually beneficial cooperation with the Member States of the Organization of Islamic Cooperation, respecting their social and political systems and traditional spiritual and moral values. In pursuing these aims, the Russian Federation is going to focus on:

1) developing the full-scale and trustful cooperation with the Islamic Republic of Iran, providing comprehensive support for the Syrian Arab Republic, and deepening the multifaceted mutually beneficial partnerships with the Republic of Turkey, the Kingdom of Saudi Arabia, the Arab Republic of Egypt and the other Member States of the Organization of Islamic Cooperation, given the extent of their sovereignty and constructiveness of their policy toward the Russian Federation;

2) establishing a sustainable comprehensive regional security and

cooperation architecture in the Middle East and North Africa, based on combining the capacities of all the states and interstate alliances of the regions, including the League of Arab States and the Gulf Cooperation Council. Russia intends to actively cooperate with all the interested states and interstate associations in order to implement Russia's Collective Security Concept for the Persian Gulf Region, viewing the implementation of this initiative as an important step toward a sustainable and comprehensive normalization of the situation in the Middle East;

3) promoting interfaith and intercultural dialogue and understanding, consolidating efforts to protect traditional spiritual and moral values, and combating Islamophobia, including via the Organization of Islamic Cooperation;

4) reconciling differences and normalizing relations among the Member States of the Organization of Islamic Cooperation, as well as between these states and their neighbours (primarily the Islamic Republic of Iran and the Arab countries, the Syrian Arab Republic and its neighbours, the Arab countries and the State of Israel), including within the efforts aimed at a comprehensive and lasting solution to the Palestinian question;

5) helping resolve and overcome consequences of armed conflicts in the Middle East, North Africa, South, Southeast Asia and other regions where Member States of the Organization of Islamic Cooperation are located;

6) unleashing the economic potential of the Member States of the Organization of Islamic Cooperation with a view to establishing the Greater Eurasian Partnership.

Africa

57. Russia stands in solidarity with the African states in their desire for a more equitable polycentric world and elimination of social and economic inequality, which is growing due to the sophisticated neo-colonial policies of some developed states towards Africa. The Russian Federation intends to support further the establishment of Africa as a distinctive and influential centre of world development, giving priority to:

1) supporting the sovereignty and independence of interested African states, including through security assistance, inter alia food and energy security, as well as military and military-technical cooperation;

2) assistance in resolving and overcoming the consequences of armed conflicts in Africa, especially inter-ethnic and ethnic ones, advocating the leading role of African states in these efforts, based on the principle 'African problems – African solution';

3) strengthening and deepening Russian-African cooperation in various

spheres on a bilateral and multilateral basis, primarily within the framework of the African Union and the Russia-Africa Partnership Forum;

4) increasing trade and investment with African states and African integration structures (primarily the African Continental Free Trade Area, the African Export-Import Bank and other leading subregional organizations), including through the EAEU;

5) promoting and developing links in the humanitarian sphere, including scientific cooperation, training of national personnel, strengthening health systems, providing other assistance, promoting intercultural dialogue, protecting traditional spiritual and moral values, and the right to freedom of religion.

Latin America and the Caribbean

58. Given the progressive strengthening of the sovereignty and multifaceted potential of Latin American and Caribbean states, the Russian Federation intends to develop relations with them on a pragmatic, de-ideologized and mutually beneficial basis, giving priority attention to:

1) supporting interested Latin American states under pressure from the United States and its allies in securing sovereignty and independence, including through the promotion and expansion of security, military and military-technical cooperation;

2) strengthening friendship, mutual understanding and deepening multifaceted mutually beneficial partnership with the Federative Republic of Brazil, the Republic of Cuba, the Republic of Nicaragua, the Bolivarian Republic of Venezuela, developing relations with other Latin American states, taking into account the degree of independence and constructiveness of their policy towards the Russian Federation;

3) increasing mutual trade and investment with Latin American and Caribbean States, including through cooperation with the Community of Latin American and Caribbean States, the Common Market of the South, the Central American Integration System, the Bolivarian Alliance for the Peoples of the Americas, the Pacific Alliance, and the Caribbean Community;

4) expanding cultural, scientific, educational, sports, tourism and other humanitarian ties with the states of the region.

European region

59. Most European states pursue an aggressive policy towards Russia aimed at creating threats to the security and sovereignty of the Russian Federation, gaining unilateral economic advantages, undermining

domestic political stability and eroding traditional Russian spiritual and moral values, and creating obstacles to Russia's cooperation with allies and partners. In this connection, the Russian Federation intends to consistently defend its national interests by giving priority attention to:

1) reducing and neutralizing threats to security, territorial integrity, sovereignty, traditional spiritual and moral values, and socio-economic development of Russia, its allies and partners from unfriendly European states, the North Atlantic Treaty Organization, the European Union and the Council of Europe;

2) creating conditions for the cessation of unfriendly actions by European states and their associations, for a complete rejection of the anti-Russian course (including interference in Russia's internal affairs) by these states and their associations, and for their transition to a long-term policy of good-neighbourliness and mutually beneficial cooperation with Russia;

3) the formation of a new model of coexistence by European states to ensure the safe, sovereign and progressive development of Russia, its allies and partners, and durable peace in the European part of Eurasia, taking into account the potential of multilateral formats, including the Organization for Security and Cooperation in Europe.

60. Objective prerequisites for the formation of a new model of coexistence with European states are geographical proximity, historically developed deep cultural, humanitarian and economic ties of the peoples and states of the European part of Eurasia. The main factor complicating the normalization of relations between Russia and European states is the strategic course of the USA and their individual allies to draw and deepen dividing lines in the European region in order to weaken and undermine the competitiveness of the economies of Russia and European states, as well as to limit the sovereignty of European states and ensure US global domination.

61. The realization by the states of Europe that there is no alternative to peaceful coexistence and mutually beneficial equal cooperation with Russia, an increase in the level of their foreign policy independence and a transition to a policy of good neighbourliness with the Russian Federation will have a positive effect on the security and welfare of the European region and help European states take their proper place in the Greater Eurasian Partnership and in a multipolar world.

The US and other Anglo-Saxon states

62. Russia's course towards the US has a combined character, taking into account the role of this state as one of the influential sovereign centres of

world development and at the same time the main inspirer, organizer and executor of the aggressive anti-Russian policy of the collective West, the source of major risks to the security of the Russian Federation, international peace, a balanced, equitable and progressive development of humanity.

63. The Russian Federation is interested in maintaining strategic parity, peaceful coexistence with the United States, and the establishment of a balance of interests between Russia and the United States, taking into account their status as major nuclear powers and special responsibility for strategic stability and international security in general. The prospects of forming such a model of US-Russian relations depend on the extent to which the United States is ready to abandon its policy of power-domination and revise its anti-Russian course in favour of interaction with Russia on the basis of the principles of sovereign equality, mutual benefit, and respect for each other's interests.

64. The Russian Federation intends to build relations with other Anglo-Saxon states depending on the degree of their willingness to abandon their unfriendly course toward Russia and to respect its legitimate interests.

Antarctica

65. Russia is interested in preserving Antarctica as a demilitarized space of peace, stability and cooperation, maintaining environmental sustainability and expanding its presence in the region. For these purposes, the Russian Federation intends to give priority attention to preservation, effective implementation and progressive development of the Antarctic Treaty System of December 1, 1959.

Challenging the rise of CORPORATE POWER in Renewable Energy

Strategic opportunities for public ownership and industrial and economic development

Dexter Whitfield

SPOKESMAN

Environmental Injustice in Renewables

What is to be done?

Dexter Whitfield

Based on original research, Dexter Whitfield's new book exposes corporate domination in the development, ownership and operation of renewable energy projects and how to challenge it. He is Director of the European Services Strategy Unit. Available from bookshops or directly from Spokesman, £18.

Crisis and opportunities

The objective of this book is to demonstrate how corporate interests dominate the renewable energy sector. They range from private investment funds, venture capital funds, private equity funds and subsidiaries of fossil fuel companies which are developers and owner-operators of wind farms, solar parks, storage, hydro and other projects.

These projects are bought and sold in the secondary market with development rights and 'construction-ready status', either as individual projects or as part of a portfolio of operational projects, often located in several countries. The analysis is based on the European Services Strategy Unit Global Renewable Energy Database which contains 1,622 transactions between 1 January 2019 and 31st December 2021.

Several publicly-owned companies in Norway, Sweden, Denmark, France, Germany, China, Romania and the Republic of Ireland are developers and owners of renewable energy assets, but the public sector is in a minority compared to the private sector in a global context.

The long-term impact is likely to be the replacement of multinational fossil fuel companies by multinational renewable energy companies in a system where market forces are dominant. The IMF and vested interests believe the public sector's role should be limited to catalysing private sector finance by taking on risk, funding research and development.

But electricity is a public good, hence it is imperative that not-for-profit publicly-owned companies have a vital role in developing, owning and operating renewable energy projects and distributing energy.

Later chapters of the book chart a way forward in which the public sector can and must have a significant and sustainable role in the provision and ownership of renewable energy projects. This includes the different forms of decarbonisation ranging from retrofitting homes, public buildings and business premises and national planning for environmental adaptations and building resilience, and requires the full application of public values and a core public values framework.

Governments also have a key role in ensuring compliance with equality and equity legislation and economic development initiatives to provide manufacturing and servicing facilities for renewable projects. They must align with the provision of training to maximise the employment opportunities afforded by the renewable energy sector. The decommodification of nature and biodiversity must equally be centre stage.

The corporatisation of renewable energy must systematically be removed and replaced by a new era of not-for-profit publicly owned organisations geared to radically transform the ownership and operation of renewable energy in a way which is participative, with rigorous scrutiny, oversight and democratic accountability.

Climate crisis context

The scientific evidence of a climate crisis overwhelmingly supports the need for decarbonisation to totally replace fossil fuels with renewable energy by 2050 (Intergovernmental Panel on Climate Change, 2021). Forecasts predict the continuing melting of glaciers, rising sea levels, flooding and coastal erosion, the rising threat of extraordinary landscape fires leading to deaths or injuries, power cuts, damage to homes, transport and agriculture.

A follow-up IPCC report examined the vulnerability, adaptation and resilience of human and natural systems and defined three principles of climate justice:

"...distributive justice which refers to the allocation of burdens and benefits among individuals, nations and generations; procedural justice which refers to who decides and participates in decision-making; and recognition which entails basic respect and robust engagement with and fair consideration of diverse cultures and perspectives" (IPCC, 2022).

Nine additional studies by agencies and research teams have upgraded the threat of rising sea levels; the risk of wildfires; the melting of glaciers; the deadly impact of pollution on the health of millions in communities; the likelihood of missing the 1.5 C target; failure to strand fossil fuel assets in the ground; and the needs of 940m people with no access to electricity and 2.6bn who need space cooling.

"By 2050, the expected relative sea level (RSL) will cause tide and storm surge heights to increase and will lead to a shift in U.S. coastal flood regimes, with major and moderate high tide flood events occurring as frequently as moderate and minor high tide flood events occur today. Without additional risk-reduction measures, U.S. coastal infrastructure, communities, and ecosystems will face significant consequences" (Global and Regional Sea Level Rise: Scenarios for the United States, National Oceanic and Atmospheric Administration, 2022).

"A wildfire results from a complex interaction of biological, meteorological, physical, and social factors that influence the likelihood of a wildfire breaking out, its propagation and intensity, duration and extent, and its potential to cause damage to economies, the environment, and society. Around the world many of these factors – climate, land use and land management practices, and demographics – are changing" (Spreading Like Wildfire: The Rising Threat of Extraordinary Landscape Fires, UNEP, 2022).

A new study calculates that, between 2000 and 2019, glaciers collectively lost around 267bn tonnes of ice every year. Assuming that all the water from melting glaciers eventually reach the ocean, this means that meltwater from glaciers alone contributed 0.74mm of sea level rise every year (Hugonnet et al, 2021). Another study found that the Arctic has warmed nearly four times faster than the globe between 1979-2021 (Rantanen et al, 2022).

"Pollution and toxic substances kill more than 9 million people per year, damage the health of billions, and inflict costs measured in trillions of dollars. Everyone in the world is affected by the pervasive pollution that characterizes life in the 21st century, even newborn infants. However, the burden of contamination falls most heavily upon communities that already are vulnerable or marginalized because of race, poverty and other socio-economic factors. This phenomenon is known as environmental injustice" (Boyd and Hadley-Burke, United Nations, 2022).

> "There is a 50:50 chance of average global temperature reaching 1.5 degrees Celcius above pre-industrial levels in the next five years, and the likelihood is increasing with time……A single year of exceedance above 1.5 °C does not mean we have breached the iconic threshold of the Paris Agreement, but it does reveal that we are edging ever closer to a situation where 1.5 °C could be exceeded for an extended period" (World Meteorological Organization, 2022).

> "We find that developed reserves of oil, gas and coal significantly exceed what can be extracted and burned within the 1.5 °C budget, a conclusion that is robust to uncertainties in reserves and carbon budgets. Given a rapidly closing window to keep warming below 1.5 °C, these findings call for urgent policy attention on managing an orderly and equitable phase-out of fossil fuel extraction" (Trout, K. et al, 2022).

> Space cooling will become increasingly important to prevent heat-related deaths and reduced productivity with global demand expected to soar 395% from 800 gigawatts in 2016 to 3,350GW in 2050 as temperatures rise and urbanisation increases to 68% of the world population living in urban areas by 2050. 2.8bn people live in hottest parts of the world but only 8% possess air conditioners in contrast to 90% ownership in USA and Japan (OECD/International Energy Agency, 2018, United Nations Environment Programme, 2022).

> "…passive building and city design and innovative cooling technologies will be needed to ensure essential cooling for all that minimize environmental damage" (Mastrucci et al, 2019).

"Extreme Danger" (Heat Index above 125 degrees F) will impact about 107m people in the USA in 2053, an increase of 13 times over 30 years thus requiring access to very significant cooling (First Street Foundation, 2022). Meanwhile,

> "…global fossil fuel subsidies were $5.9 trillion or 6.8 percent of GDP in 2020 and are expected to increase to 7.4 percent of GDP in 2025 as the share of fuel consumption in emerging markets (where price gaps are generally larger) continues to climb" (IMF, 2021).

Direct and indirect subsidies comprised under-pricing local air pollution costs (42%), global warming costs (29%), congestion and road accidents

(15%), explicit subsidies (8%) and foregone consumption tax revenue (6%). In addition,

> "...in 2020 and 2021, the EIB provided almost €2 billion in loans to companies with a high share of coal in their power and heat generation portfolios" (Counter Balance, 2022).

Even more important is the destruction of nation states, the mass killing of people of all ages and deliberate indiscriminate demolition of cities and towns and their public infrastructure of hospitals, schools, public transport, housing and local economies by despots. Others persecute minority groups on an industrial scale. There are current wars or conflicts in Ukraine, Yemen, Sudan, Ethiopia and earlier ones in Syria, Afghanistan, Myanmar, Iraq, Libya, plus civil wars and territorial disputes in several countries.

The Russian invasion of Ukraine in February 2022 led to global financial sanctions and withdrawal from corporate contracts and projects. Germany accelerated implementation of the Renewable Energy Sources Act (EEG) and plans for renewables to account for 80% of its electricity needs by 2030 and 100% by 2035. The Nord Stream 2 Russian gas pipeline which was designed to double gas supply to Germany was blocked and later blown up.

US Supreme Court 6-3 decision in June 2022 on West Virginia v. Environmental Protection Agency ruled that Agency has very limited powers to regulate power plant emission of greenhouse gases under a provision of the Clean Air Act or to force polluting plants to close. *The New York Times* described it as:

> "...the product of a coordinated, multiyear strategy by Republican attorneys general, conservative legal activists and their funders to use the judicial system to rewrite environmental law, weakening the executive branch's ability to tackle global warming" (Andreoni, 2022).

The decision will empower corporations to slow emission reduction and means the transition process to 2050 will be even more conflictual.

Figure 1 indicates two important realities. Firstly, the high level of regional dependency on coal, oil and natural gas. Secondly, the low level of energy consumption through renewables. Wind and solar power provided 10.2% of energy generation in 2021, exceeding 10% for the first time (British Petroleum, 2022).

Figure 1: The level of coal, oil and natural gas dependency

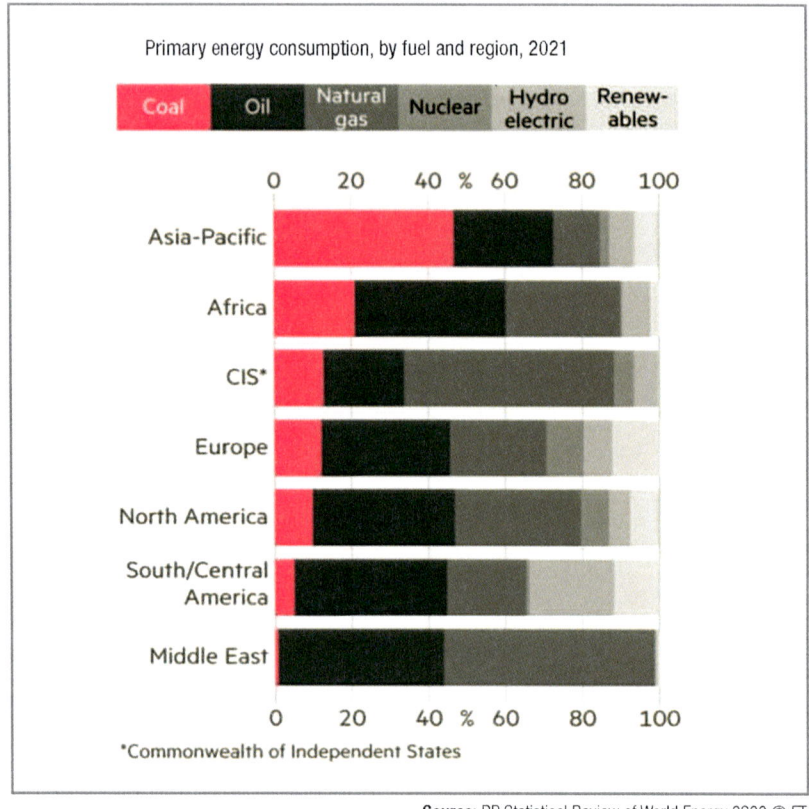

Source: BP Statistical Review of World Energy 2022 © FT

The chart exposes the scale of transformation required over the next three decades to meet the climate targets and environmental adaptation and protection. It indicates the limited progress to date and continued reliance on markets, market forces and the corporate sector. More of the same is almost certain to be a disaster with profound climate, environmental, economic and human impacts.

To achieve decarbonisation by 2050 will require 816GW of wind and 632GW of solar installed every year to 2050, plus 257GWh battery storage per annum according to a global forecast (BloombergNEF, 2021). The forecast assumes 49% of electricity will be used to produce large quantities of hydrogen with the remainder by end users in the economy. The forecast implies current investment will have to double – for example annual investment of US$1.7 trillion in 2020 will have to increase to between US$3.1 and US$5.8 trillion every year for three decades (ibid).

In this context it is critically important to identify the structural flaws in the current provision of renewable energy and to map the transformative changes required to achieve the climate targets and an equitable transition.

Structural flaws

The key characteristics of the renewable energy sector are summarised below and are supported by the evidence in the ESSU Global Renewable Energy Secondary Market Database 2019-2021.

- There were 1,622 transactions of renewable energy assets in the 3-year period between 1 January 2019 to 31 December 2021; the high level of secondary market sale of wind, solar, hydro, battery, storage, biomass and energy-from-waste projects together with corporate takeovers and partnerships in the development stage of projects. Market ideology and market interests dominate the sector and outsourcing is widespread.
- The twelve major publicly owned renewable energy companies plus three major companies that have a minority public shareholding collectively own 1,671 projects with 98.5GW operational capacity or 3.47% of the global total.
- Public sector organisations bought and sold assets in the secondary market in the same period via 79 acquisitions and 41 sales accounting for 24.6GW. Whilst the acquisitions increased the overall public sector owned GW by 37.9GW, this was countered by the sale of assets by the public sector reducing power generation by 24.6GW. This resulted in a mere 0.46% or 13.6GW increase in public sector renewable energy generating power to 3.93%.
- Private Equity Funds have carved out a pivotal role financing and owning renewable energy assets – they acquired 369 renewable energy assets and sold 178 projects between 2019-2021.
- 41 major renewable energy companies registered in tax havens were involved in 264 transactions to acquire assets whilst a further 47 transactions involved the sale of renewable energy assets. The use of tax havens to avoid or reduce corporate taxation increases corporate profits but reduces tax revenue for governments.
- A sample of 20 private renewable energy companies paid their shareholders US$10.7bn in dividends in 2021 alone. In addition, eight fossil fuel multinational corporations had total profits of US$67.71bn in the second quarter of 2022.
- Pension funds have increased ownership of renewable energy assets – 17 pension funds were involved in 39 transactions that acquired renewable energy projects with 43,476MW and 8 transactions that sold projects with 7,213MW.

- Democratic accountability is weak with limited community participation and a lack of scrutiny/oversight and rigorous and comprehensive economic, social and environmental evaluation and impact assessment.
- Environment, Social and Governance (ESG) is widely promoted but is totally inadequate in terms of equalities, employment, social, economic and environmental justice, democratic accountability and transparency.
- Despite the wide criticism and failure of many Public Private Partnership projects, the World Bank and regional development banks continue to promote the PPP model for renewable energy projects in the global south.
- The cost of transactions was disclosed for 504 transactions (31.07%) and totalled US$206,723m, on the basis that these transactions were a representative sample of all 1,622 transactions the total cost was US$671.8bn. Legal and technical transaction costs were estimated to be US$15.0bn, giving the overall cost of the secondary market in renewable energy in the 2019-2021 period to be US$686.8bn.
- The sector is increasingly globalised as many renewable energy companies, developers, financial institutions, constructors and operators traverse nation state boundaries.
- Significant technological advances have been achieved in solar panels, floating offshore wind farms, turbines, battery storage and tidal technology. The rate of innovation and technological development are likely to accelerate leading to new models of renewable energy such as tidal power, more powerful battery storage and efficiency/effectiveness improvements in solar and wind turbines and blades.
- The hedge fund Elliott Management, known for buying the debt of developing economies at knock-down prices and then suing governments for full payment of the debt, targeted three energy companies in 2019-2021 – EDP (Portugal), Duke Energy Corporation (USA) and SSE (UK and Ireland). Elliott acquired company shares and sought to persuade the respective board of directors to sell off subsidiaries or to 'maximise shareholder value' which would benefit Elliott. It failed.

Key objectives

To focus attention on renewable energy generation and the related trends and developments including the trade in assets, mergers and acquisitions, joint ventures and partnerships in the secondary market.

To investigate the global scale of the sale of operational renewable energy assets such as wind, solar, hydro, biomass, energy-from-waste and battery storage projects in the secondary market to reveal the scale of tax avoidance in their planning, finance, construction and operation.

To identify the extensive role of the private sector, particularly private equity funds, in the renewable energy sector and their wide use of tax havens. This has far-reaching implications because the current corporate ownership and control of the fossil fuel industry could be replicated in the renewable energy sector by 2050 or earlier.

To de-commodify and reverse the marketisation, corporatisation and privatisation of the renewable energy sector and to rapidly increase public sector capabilities to plan, develop, own, operate and manage renewable energy projects.

To integrate the continued expansion of renewable energy with an industrial strategy involving local/regional manufacture and production, the manufacture of retrofitting plant and materials together with the equipment and material required for environmental adaptation and protection.

To develop a comprehensive action plan for public ownership, provision and democratic accountability including Net Zero Economic Zones to city scale, industrial hub or local areas, city centres or neighbourhoods, large scale retrofitting, alternative uses for sites and factories to promote local/regional economic development and employment. This will include developing job and skills training for all of these tasks and to plan, coordinate and deliver retrofitting and undertake future repair, maintenance and upgrades.

To expose the limitations of ESG and set out an alternative framework of public values inclusive of the dimensions of equality, social, economic, labour and environmental justice.

To expose the methods that are being adopted to financialise, commercialise and privatise nature and biodiversity and to emphasize the need to focus on sustaining their role and their contribution in sustaining and enhancing their role.

To identify the scope for corporate disruption combined with building alliances of workers and trade unions, community organisations, political parties and NGOs to draw up proposals for renewable energy and retrofitting projects that meet their needs for power under local planning, control and accountability.

To emphasize the need for the integration of nature and biodiversity, sustainable objectives, good quality jobs, regeneration and economic change aligned with equality and public values across the renewable energy and decarbonisation agendas.

To stress the importance for governments, international organisations, political parties and trade unions to use the extensive evidence of the poor performance and impact of PPP projects to make the case for publicly-owned and operated projects in developing economies.

Robert Green (right) with Robert McNamara and Lee Butler in Tokyo in 1999

How John Ainslie influenced my life

Commander Robert Green Royal Navy (Ret'd)

Commander Green reflects on John Ainslie's influence on his own progress from nuclear warrior to committed campaigner for nuclear disarmament. Spokesman 153 (Bairns not Bombs) compiled selected works by John Ainslie. Commander Green is the author of Security without Nuclear Deterrence *(Spokesman £17.99).*

On 15 May 1992, I found myself in a conference room in the UN Palais des Nations, Geneva, crowded with over a hundred delegates from 32 countries. Just over a year earlier, I had spoken out against nuclear deterrence to 20,000 anti-Gulf War demonstrators from the plinth of Nelson's Column in Trafalgar Square. Maybe this was a fitting soapbox for a former bombardier-navigator who flew in nuclear-capable Buccaneer strike jets with a target in Russia in 1968-72 and then, until 1977, in anti-submarine helicopters able to drop nuclear depth-bombs. Promoted to Commander in 1978, I had worked in the Ministry of Defence as personal staff officer to the Admiral responsible for UK nuclear weapon policy under Margaret Thatcher, before my final job as Staff Officer (Intelligence) to the Commander in Chief Fleet, Admiral Sir John Fieldhouse, who ran the 1982 Falklands War from a bunker under northwest London.

Ten years later, having broken free from my pro-nuclear deterrence indoctrination, I was now leading a 12-strong British delegation as the recently elected Chair of the UK affiliate of the World Court Project (WCP). We had come to Geneva to support the international launch of this project, pioneering a network of anti-nuclear civil society organisations campaigning to outlaw nuclear deterrence by requesting an Advisory Opinion from the International Court of Justice (ICJ) in The Hague on the legality of the threat or use of nuclear weapons. The campaign had gained serious traction after the International Association of Lawyers Against Nuclear Arms (IALANA), International Physicians for the

Prevention of Nuclear War (IPPNW), Nobel Peace Prize winners in 1985, and the International Peace Bureau (IPB), inaugural Nobel Peace laureates in 1892, had teamed up as World Court Project co-sponsors, coordinated from the IPB's headquarters in Geneva.

The scheduled speakers included Petra Kelly, charismatic leader of the German Green Party. However, she had just withdrawn following a suspicious hit and run attack by a taxi injuring her partner, ex-General Gert Bastian. At short notice, therefore, the organisers had asked Kate Dewes, a leading peace and disarmament campaigner from Aotearoa/New Zealand (A/NZ), to take her place.

I became entranced as Kate spoke quietly but strongly how she had been inspired by another keynote speaker, the distinguished US international law expert, Dr Richard Falk. Back in 1986 she had been coordinating the South Island branch of the Peace Foundation and organised for Falk to speak in support of what became, the following year, A/NZ's iconic nuclear-free policy. Under the inspiring leadership of Labour Prime Minister David Lange, this policy was placed on the statute book in 1987.

Falk had sown the seed of the campaign for retired Christchurch magistrate Harold Evans to pioneer a legal challenge to nuclear deterrence, and sound out support among fellow lawyers in A/NZ and Australia. Following the Geneva launch, an International Steering Committee was formed with Kate and myself as A/NZ and UK representatives respectively; and over the subsequent weekend we learned more about each other.

A month later back in UK, I received a letter from Kate with the envelope disturbingly slit open at one end. A Special Committee on Nuclear Propulsion had been appointed by A/NZ's conservative government following US and UK pressure to repeal A/NZ's unique nuclear-free legislation. The Committee had been hearing evidence about the hazards of visits by nuclear-powered warships, and things were not going well for the objectors. Kate asked if I could provide any UK evidence to strengthen their case.

Cue John Ainslie's entry into our lives. Fortuitously, I had just received a copy of John's first, powerful report for Scottish CND, *Cracking Under Pressure*, on information he had uncovered about hairline cracks found in the stainless steel propulsion reactor cooling pipes of UK nuclear submarines, including the Polaris force. The UK Government had been sufficiently concerned to set up a Nuclear-Powered Warships Safety Committee to investigate and recommend how to fix the problem.

Kate wrote that not only had the A/NZ Special Committee not seen

John's report: despite an expensive "fact-finding" visit to UK, they had not even met the Nuclear-Powered Warships Safety Committee.

In 1992, British investigative journalist David Leigh had a regular current affairs programme on Thames TV; and by chance I watched it in May when he featured John's report, headlining the programme 'Polaris in Deep Water'. Leigh interviewed Reg Farmer, spokesman for the UK Nuclear-Powered Warships Safety Committee, who admitted the reactor problem. He then revealed that consequently UK nuclear submarines had been banned from foreign port visits – but not to British ports.

When I phoned Thames TV, they were happy to mail a copy of the interview transcript to me. It arrived in a normal looking A4 envelope; however, on opening it I found that pages 15-23 covering Farmer's admission had been ripped off the staple and were missing.

On informing Thames TV, they replied: 'Oh dear, it's happened again; we'll send another copy, and a video by registered mail.' These reached me undamaged. Having photocopied the full transcript, I sent it, the video and a copy of John's report to Kate by courier. She immediately sent copies of these to ex-PM David Lange, who reported later that the video went missing off his desk.

She was so impressed by the material that she invited me on behalf of the A/NZ anti-nuclear movement for a three-week speaking tour from 20 August-9 September about all aspects of nuclearism, and to help promote the World Court Project. Amazingly, in just over two weeks she raised enough money to cover my flight tickets.

I brought with me the incomplete Thames TV transcript: this plus the full version and programme video became potent visual aids when explaining nuclear power's incompatibility with democracy. When I landed in Auckland I found a second spring with daffodils bursting into bloom, lambing just started, and a warm Kiwi welcome.

Kate proved to be a phenomenal organiser and minder. My first public meeting at Auckland University launched the A/NZ WCP public awareness campaign. This was a heady experience, sharing a platform with David Lange and Dr Robin Briant, a leading IPPNW spokeswoman. Meetings followed in all the main centres of this beautiful nuclear-free Garden of Eden; moreover, I discovered it has no snakes!

Three highlights stood out. In the capital Wellington, the public meeting audience included the French Defence Attaché, representatives from the Russian, Chinese and Malaysian missions, and a serving Commander from the A/NZ Defence Department. The second high point was a 45-minute meeting with an uncomfortable Minister for Disarmament and Justice,

Douglas Graham. (Could one imagine such a UK Cabinet post?) The third was at the University of Canterbury, when I confronted Sir Edward Somers, Chairman of the Special Committee on Nuclear Propulsion, with John Ainslie's report.

Trying to lighten the tense atmosphere, I bantered that his committee seemed to be 'the only ones in step', as my RN parade training instructor at Dartmouth used to bellow while drilling us young officers. Then I berated him that his committee should be proudly protecting their country's nuclear-free status from the predations of an all-powerful, ruthless international nuclear industry.

While visiting Nelson during the speaking tour, I made a grim pilgrimage to Lord Ernest Rutherford's birthplace. A slightly kitsch memorial had recently been erected there, sponsored by companies involved with the nuclear industry (https://shorturl.at/btuI6). It comprised an inclined walkway lined with panels covering Rutherford's life and achievements, spiralling up to a rather disturbing central sculpture depicting the world's first nuclear scientific superstar as a studious young boy.

At the end of each talk I posed a challenge: could the nation which nurtured this man who first split the atom lead the world into the post-nuclear era? Audiences responded positively, fired up by my terrible cautionary tale about the nuclear blind alley with its incestuous link between power generation and weapons, whereby a by-product of power plants is fissile material for bombs. Both have proved grotesquely costly and ineffective providers, respectively, of electricity and security.

Over the next four years, Kate and I attended meetings of the International Steering Committee of the World Court Project in the US and Europe. In 1994, A/NZ was among very few Western UN member States that voted for a General Assembly resolution — which the five permanent Security Council members could not prevent — requesting an advisory opinion from the International Court of Justice. This passed comfortably with strong support from the 110-member states Non-Aligned Movement. On 8 July 1996, I was in the International Court of Justice at The Hague when its 14 judges delivered their historic judgment confirming the general illegality of the threat, let alone use, of nuclear weapons.

The following January, Kate and I were married in Christchurch; however, I had to return to the UK to lead a new campaign promoting the Court's decision, and look after my father with whom I was living following divorce from my first wife. When he died in 1999, I emigrated to join Kate and her three daughters.

Anticipating these life-changing developments, two years before we had seen the need for an influential A/NZ centre promoting alternative security thinking coherent with the nuclear-free legislation to challenge increasingly regressive US, UK and Australian defence policies, at a time of cutbacks in peace research centres. In September 1997, therefore, we established a Disarmament & Security Centre (DSC), with Kate and myself as Coordinators in our Christchurch home.

When I emigrated in 1999, we combined my extensive UK archive with Kate's unique documentary record of A/NZ disarmament and peace work since 1975. The DSC provided a resource centre for legislators, decision-makers, historians, academics, students and activists. Our complementary strengths gave us the credibility to apply for international funding to maintain the DSC and fund our intensive international travel on Track Two (backchannel) diplomatic missions.

In 1998, Canadian former Senator Douglas Roche appointed me as Chair of his newly formed Middle Powers Initiative (MPI) Strategic Planning Committee, with Kate a member. Over the next five years, we positioned MPI as an influential non-governmental organisation complementing the New Agenda Coalition, formed earlier that year by the Foreign Ministers of Brazil, Egypt, Ireland, Mexico, New Zealand, South Africa, and Sweden as an 'across-the-blocs' anti-nuclear response to the alarming announcements of India and Pakistan's acquisition of nuclear weapons. We helped organise and run several strategy consultations, held in prestigious venues like the Rockefeller Foundation, New York; and I led several delegations to key NATO member states including Norway and Germany, as well as Australia and Japan. My apotheosis in this role came in November 1999 when I led an MPI delegation to Tokyo comprising the supreme duo of chastened anti-nuclear converts, Robert McNamara and General Lee Butler USAF (Ret).

In 2000, John Ainslie swung my attention back to nuclear submarine propulsion hazards. Another small crack had been found in the primary cooling circuit of the reactor in the UK nuclear attack submarine (SSN) HMS *Tireless*, causing all *Trafalgar* and *Swiftsure* class SSNs to be recalled; but apparently the four new *Vanguard* class Trident-armed submarines were unaffected.

John Ainslie made a transcript of an extraordinary BBC Radio 4 'File on 4' programme on 12 December 2000, when *Tireless*'s engineers recounted what happened when the crack was found while deployed in the Mediterranean. Some highlights from John's transcript follow:

To see where the fault was, crew members had to enter the reactor compartment itself where there might be a radiation hazard... The escape of water was at a critical junction in the cooling system on the wrong side of safety valves which can isolate and stop leaks from other parts of the pipework — the worst place says the Navy for a leak to occur.

The reactor was put through a rapid shutdown, called a SCRAM. The engineers found they could not stop the leak, but it was small; so they advised their Commanding Officer to risk restarting the reactor so that the submarine could get to the nearest repair facility in Gibraltar as soon as possible ... After 36 hours, the reactor was shut down again to inspect the leak: it was growing, so it was shut down for good... Tireless continued slowly to Gibraltar under auxiliary diesel power. After it docked, a nuclear safety team including independent consultant John Large advised on the likely repairs needed: he criticised the decision to risk restarting the reactor.

Tireless sat in dock in Gibraltar awaiting repair, causing growing unease among the local population. Spanish authorities watched from across the bay in Algeciras, drawing unwelcome attention to Gibraltar's anachronistic status as one of the last British colonial possessions. Repairs took a year, during which just one SSN was operationally available.

Checks revealed that a total of seven out of 12 of the SSN fleet had signs of cracking at the same critical junction in their reactor cooling system. All seven were withdrawn from service for repairs, while the other five were said not to have the problem.

The sad saga of the successor *Astute* class SSN programme highlights anxieties about a viable future for the Submarine Service. This is despite recent excitement over the AUKUS deal to provide SSNs for Australia which, because of its exorbitant cost and daunting technical and personnel challenges involving massive US support, is inevitably doomed.

In 2002 *Astute*'s construction was three years behind and several hundred million pounds over budget: 200 US designers and managers, including a new project director, had to be brought in to help. Launched in 2007, HMS *Astute*'s problems included design flaws, unreliable equipment and poor construction; and her cost rocketed to almost £1.4bn. The last of the *Swiftsure* class had to be scrapped in 2010; and *Astute* class delays meant that in 2012 just five SSNs were operational.

John Ainslie monitored reports of a further accident in 2013 in *Tireless* when reactor coolant again leaked for eight days while off the west coast of Scotland. Finally decommissioned in 2014, she joined 18 other nuclear submarines awaiting dismantling. With the first UK SSN HMS *Dreadnought* still rusting in Rosyth since 1980, the cost of keeping them there and in Devonport is rising and space running out, as the Ministry of Defence struggles to find an environmentally safe and cost-effective means of disposal. The daunting extent of what is entailed can be gauged by the experience of the US Navy (https://shorturl.at/orILM).

As the UK Government and Royal Navy anxiously persist with the new, increasingly US dependent *Dreadnought* class to replace the Trident-armed *Vanguard* class submarine force, the Submarine Service is leaving a dark, irresponsible legacy of radioactive contamination for future generations to resolve, and a barely viable surface Fleet.

Meanwhile, I salute dear John, and pay tribute to his crucial influence in bringing me to my current peaceful dotage, enjoying watching six step-grandchildren aged from 14 years to two months grow up in our nuclear-free haven.

Security *without* Nuclear Deterrence

By Commander Robert Green, Royal Navy (Ret'd)

Foreword by Vice Admiral Sir Jeremy Blackham KCB MA

"One of the best informed and most searching critiques of the central strategic doctrine of the nuclear age – nuclear deterrence – that I know of."

Jonathan Schell, author of *The Fate of the Earth*, Yale University

£17.99 | 266 pages | Paperback

www.spokesmanbooks.org

The Mistake

A drama on the beginning of the nuclear age by Michael Mears

Claudia Delpero

Claudia Delpero edits Europe Street News (europestreet.news). She saw the play at the Arcola Theatre in London in February 2023.

'An atomic bomb doesn't just fall, someone has to drop it,' is the testimony of an 80-year-old woman who lost her husband in Hiroshima, in 1945. Nomura Shigeko, a young woman at that time, interpreted by British-born Japanese actress Emiko Ishii, repeats that statement on stage with all the exasperation of a survivor.

The responsibility for that bomb, it turns out, was not just with the person who dropped it, but also with several others whom Michael Mears, author and lead performer, brings together in his play *The Mistake*.

Powerful and heart stopping, *The Mistake* explores the circumstances that led to the dropping of the first nuclear bomb, a catastrophe close to the end of World War Two. The action takes place in Budapest, Berlin, London, Chicago, Washington, Long Island, Tinian Island and Hiroshima, with Michael Mears brilliantly interpreting the key figures involved.

He is the ingenious Hungarian-German-American scientist Leo Szilard, inventor of the bomb, and daring General Paul Tibbets, pilot of the plane who dropped it. He is also Albert Einstein, who alerted US President Franklin Delano Roosevelt that Nazi Germany was attempting to build an atomic weapon; Enrico Fermi and Robert Oppenheimer, the physicists who participated in the creation of the first nuclear reactor and nuclear test explosions; and President Roosevelt himself, who greenlighted the project.

Michael Mears has been working as an actor for four decades, in theatre, film and television. He has written and performed three solo plays for the stage and seven for

BBC Radio 4. His 1990s show about homelessness, *Soup*, won *The Scotsman* Fringe First Award at the Edinburgh Festival. He performed his more recent play, *This Evil Thing*, about Britain's World War One conscientious objectors, more than 100 times across Britain and the United States. He film and television appearances include *Four Weddings and a Funeral*, *Little Dorrit*, *The Good Soldier Schwejk* and *Last Night in Soho*, as well as *Parade's End*, *Sanditon* and *The Crown*.

Michael decided to explore the topic of nuclear weapons in 2002. On the anniversary of the Hiroshima bombing that year, he read two interviews in *The Guardian*: one with General Paul Tibbets, the other with poet Fumiko Miura, a survivor of the second atomic bomb, launched over Nagasaki a few days after the first one at Hiroshima.

'I thought it would be fascinating to think of a drama where the elderly pilot meets a survivor and is confronted with what he did,' Mears says.

He started to research the project and to take inspiration from the journal of a survivor. But it was only around the 75th anniversary of the end of World War Two, in 2020, that the idea took shape.

'The Hungarian scientist discovering the nuclear chain reaction, Leo Szilard, was fascinating to me. He was a brilliant physicist, passionate about science and experimentation but at the same time he was really anti-war. There was a complete revolution in his thinking that this weapon should never be used and yet he helped to build it. He had guilt about what he had done, whereas the pilot had not. There are these two contrasting male roles, alongside the story of the female survivor, so building and dropping the bomb are dovetailed with its actual effect,' Mears adds.

'The other thing I learnt is that this is a complex story and it is not black and white. Learning how difficult the military mission was, the meticulousness with which it was prepared, the skills and commitment it required was eye opening. You sort of respect the persons even though you disagree with them,' he continues.

'Probably my biggest insight is that people's motives are rarely straightforward, they are often complex, involving all kinds of deals and compromises with themselves. There are no villains – only people doing what they believe to be right at the time. But sometimes what they believe is right can lead to catastrophic consequences for others.'

The narrative of the play reflects this complexity linking science, politics and personal stories. It is informative, as it explains events without being one-sided. It is moving as it connects history to life and the emotions of the people who were at the centre of it. It also leaves the audience with many questions, topics for discussion and probably a desire to know more.

Do we need war to appreciate peace? Do we need a tragedy of these proportions – the two atomic bombings killed between 129,000 and 226,000 people – to bring an end to war? What other technologies is science developing that could be used with fatal consequences by 'mistake'?

'On a broader scale, it is my hope that the play, as well as being a dramatic and moving theatrical experience, will also provoke debate, informed debate. I am a pacifist and I hope that audience members who are not opposed to nuclear weapons will think more deeply about what this entails and what the prospects of a nuclear conflagration would mean for the planet. Above all, I hope that the play will change the hearts and minds of those who are not convinced about nuclear disarmament – and strengthen the hearts and minds of those who are,' says Michal Mears.

The Mistake was performed twice in London in July 2022, at the Edinburgh Festival in August 2022, and again in London, at the Arcola Theatre, in February 2023. It returned to the Arcola in April, and will tour Britain in the autumn of 2023.

The Mistake — Upcoming dates

September
Fri 8th Dartington, Devon, Studio 1 (to be confirmed)
Tue 12th Chester, Wesley Methodist Church
Wed 13th Caernarfon (NW Wales), Galeri Theatre
Thu 14th Aberystwyth Arts Centre (West Wales)
Sat 16th Wickenby, Lincolnshire, Broadbent Theatre
Wed 20th Stratford-on-Avon, Bearpit
Thu 21st Cardiff, Sherman Theatre Studio
Fri 22nd Sibford School, Banbury
Sat 23rd Walton-on-Thames, Riverhouse Barn Arts Centre
Sun 24th Chichester Arts Centre
Thu 28th Hull, Hull Truck Studio
Fri 29th Cambridge, Corpus Playroom (7pm)
Sat 30th Cambridge, Corpus Playroom (7pm)

October
Wed 4th Doncaster, McAuley Catholic High School
Thu 5th Pontefract, Ackworth Quaker School
Sat 7th York, Theatre Royal Studio
Tue 10th York, Bootham Quaker School

Wed 11th Bewdley Festival
Thu 12th Midland Arts Centre, Birmingham, Hexagon Theatre
Fri 13th Northampton, Royal and Derngate — Underground
Sat 14th Northampton, Royal and Derngate — Underground
Tue 17th Birmingham, St. Thomas Aquinas Catholic School
Thu 19th Diss, Corn Hall
Fri 20th Aldeburgh, Jubilee Hall
Sat 21st Bury St. Edmunds, Quaker Meeting House
Mon 30th Canterbury Festival

Other dates may be added including, possibly, in Berlin.
michaelmears.org

Szilard Petition to President Truman ▶

In July 1945, Leo Szilard and 69 co-signers from the Manhattan Project wrote to US President Truman asking him to consider his moral responsibilities when deciding to use the atomic bomb. They wrote:

'The development of atomic power will provide the nations with new means of destruction. The atomic bombs at our disposal represent only the first step in this direction, and there is almost no limit to the destructive power which will become available in the course of their future development.'

The efforts of Szilard's and other scientists associated with the Manhattan Project did not prevent Truman from authorising use of atomic bombs on the Japanese cities of Hiroshima and Nagasaki in August 1945. Nevertheless, Szilard and other scientists continued their campaign to warn the world of the dangers presented by atomic weapons and the opening of the atomic age. Szilard continued to probe the moral implications of the atomic and nuclear age in his writings and research. His short story collection, *The Voice of the Dolphins*, provides fascinating insights of relevance today.

Image source: http://www.dannen.com/decision/index.html

July 17, 1945

A PETITION TO THE PRESIDENT OF THE UNITED STATES

Discoveries of which the people of the United States are not aware may affect the welfare of this nation in the near future. The liberation of atomic power which has been achieved places atomic bombs in the hands of the Army. It places in your hands, as Commander-in-Chief, the fateful decision whether or not to sanction the use of such bombs in the present phase of the war against Japan.

We, the undersigned scientists, have been working in the field of atomic power. Until recently we have had to fear that the United States might be attacked by atomic bombs during this war and that her only defense might lie in a counterattack by the same means. Today, with the defeat of Germany, this danger is averted and we feel impelled to say what follows:

The war has to be brought speedily to a successful conclusion and attacks by atomic bombs may very well be an effective method of warfare. We feel, however, that such attacks on Japan could not be justified, at least not unless the terms which will be imposed after the war on Japan were made public in detail and Japan were given an opportunity to surrender.

If such public announcement gave assurance to the Japanese that they could look forward to a life devoted to peaceful pursuits in their homeland and if Japan still refused to surrender our nation might then, in certain circumstances, find itself forced to resort to the use of atomic bombs. Such a step, however, ought not to be made at any time without seriously considering the moral responsibilities which are involved.

The development of atomic power will provide the nations with new means of destruction. The atomic bombs at our disposal represent only the first step in this direction, and there is almost no limit to the destructive power which will become available in the course of their future development. Thus a nation which sets the precedent of using these newly liberated forces of nature for purposes of destruction may have to bear the responsibility of opening the door to an era of devastation on an unimaginable scale.

If after this war a situation is allowed to develop in the world which permits rival powers to be in uncontrolled possession of these new means of destruction, the cities of the United States as well as the cities of other nations will be in continuous danger of sudden annihilation. All the resources of the United States, moral and material, may have to be mobilized to prevent the advent of such a world situation. Its prevention is at present the solemn responsibility of the United States--singled out by virtue of her lead in the field of atomic power.

The added material strength which this lead gives to the United States brings with it the obligation of restraint and if we were to violate this obligation our moral position would be weakened in the eyes of the world and in our own eyes. It would then be more difficult for us to live up to our responsibility of bringing the unloosened forces of destruction under control.

In view of the foregoing, we, the undersigned, respectfully petition: first, that you exercise your power as Commander-in-Chief, to rule that the United States shall not resort to the use of atomic bombs in this war unless the terms which will be imposed upon Japan have been made public in detail and Japan knowing these terms has refused to surrender; second, that in such an event the question whether or not to use atomic bombs be decided by you in the light of the considerations presented in this petition as well as all the other moral responsibilities which are involved.

Frightful Syllogism

Günther Anders

The philosopher Günther Anders (1902-1992) left Germany for the United States as a refugee from the Nazi regime in 1933. He settled in Vienna after the war where he was to play a pioneering role in anti-nuclear activism. Anders was a member of the International War Crimes Tribunal on Vietnam. His work has an enduring relevance for those concerned with the past, present and future of humanity.

In Honour of Bertrand Russell

Günther Anders spoke at the memorial meeting, Honour Bertrand Russell – Carry on his work!, *organised by the Bertrand Russell Peace Foundation on 13th March 1970, a few weeks after Russell's death. Anders' comments were published in* The Spokesman No. 3, May 1970.

"So long as I live", Bertrand Russell wrote in his description of the beginnings of the Foundation, "I shall continue the search for means of survival of the human species, and in all probability I shall leave the work to be continued by others." Here we are, the "others", ready to continue. Here we are, and the situation in which we find ourselves requires our going on even more urgently than at the time when Russell spoke his words. The call is more urgent now than ever before.

A quarter of a century has elapsed since the dropping of the Hiroshima bomb. What in reality has become a daily and hourly peril of repetition seems to have shrunk to a chapter in a history book; and it seems to have become an utterly unreal danger, as it has never been repeated. As a matter of fact, today people are indifferent when they hear the word "atomic bomb". Their indolence, which at first, twenty-five years ago, was caused by ignorance and by lack of fantasy, seems now to be caused by sheer boredom. Since up to now – thus runs the frightful syllogism – the nuclear war has not broken out, why should it break out tomorrow? Or why should it break out at all?

Psychologically, of course, the existence of this syllogism is understandable;

logically, however, this syllogism is the purest nonsense. And even worse. For the situation deteriorates from day to day. Despite the fact that a few days ago the non-proliferation treaty was signed by the two main atomic powers, the danger for mankind is increasing steadily. And this for three reasons:

1. Because now nuclear weapons (if a means of universal suicide can be called a "weapon") lie in many hands – which means that the delicate equilibrium of the two monsters threatening but not touching each other has been disturbed.

2. New means of mass liquidation have been invented and already have been produced in over-kill quantities: therefore we cannot afford to confine ourselves to fighting atomic weapons, their stockpiling and their testing; the bacteriological and chemical weapons now at the disposal of practically every power, even the least powerful ones, are no less suicidal; and their control is not only far more difficult than that of atomic weapons, but absolutely impossible.

3. Finally, last not least, it is undeniable that every war, however small it may be at its inception, can always degenerate into an A.B.C. war, particularly if and when the technically superior aggressor fails to reach victory with so-called "conventional" weapons.

As a matter of fact, not only is such a war raging today, the one in Vietnam, but this war of liquidation, which President Nixon had promised to liquidate as fast as possible, has expanded and now even in official reports has become a war against Laos and threatens to become a war of such proportions that its sudden degeneration into a total war is far from impossible. The situation is frightful, exactly the kind of situation which Russell was never able to face without trying immediately to do something about it, and this means: something against it.

Friends, if our Bertrand Russell had reached his biblical age, it was because he felt that he could not leave the world in the lurch ... because he felt a centre of resistance had to continue to exist. For many years he successfully forbade death to enter the house of his life, in order to prevent death from entering the house of mankind. Time and again his force of life was nourished by his never ceasing indignation, by his indignation about the blind, the infamous, the indolent, the lazy, the stupid, and those incurably lacking in fantasy. The weaknesses and the vices of the others kept him alive, kept him aflame. When he was ninety, he wrote: "I become more and more of a rebel", and he goes on: "A minority, however though a growing one, feels as I do, and so long as I live it is with them that I must work."

Friends, we are this minority. And we, the minority, must not remain a minority. Through never tiring education and enlightenment of the blind and the indolent, we must become a majority, the majority, so that this majority be saved, so that all of us be saved. And not only all those must be saved who are alive today, not only all of our contemporaries, but with them also all the generations to come, tomorrow and the day after tomorrow. And among those whom we have to save are also those who have lived before us, our parents, and the whole past of our civilisation. They, too, depend upon us. For once there is no one left to remember the past, there is no past left, there has never been the past.

Therefore let us vary his words and pledge: "So long as we live, we will work in his spirit so that others will live after us, sons and daughters and their sons and daughters, and so that the effort of the former generations have not been in vain. Future and past lie in our hands. In the name of the future and the past, let us continue the work of the great old man, let us continue the work of Bertrand Russell."

* * *

Victims of Aggression

This article first appeared in Essays on Socialist Humanism in Honour of The Centenary of Bertrand Russell *(1972). It mainly relates to the US war on Vietnam, which is again in the public eye.*

The belief that today's aggressors wish to crown their aggression with victories is naive. To win wars is no longer the aim of those who are eager to wage wars – at least not for those who make the prosperity of their country depend upon their armament industry. What American industry demands, in order to guarantee the continuation of its arms production, and, thereby, the continuation of the nation's prosperity, is to *have* wars. Wars are the basis of the industrialist's power. If this basis collapsed – and it would collapse through the victorious conclusion of a war – this power would be defeated. In other words: in the present stage of capitalism, *wars as such are victories*. Victories, in the old-fashioned sense of the word, would amount to defeats, since they would promote a situation in which the further production of weapons (the prerequisite of power and prosperity) would become superfluous. What the US desires is the smooth continuity and escalation of the sale and consumption of armaments, a continuity and escalation just as regular and just as reliable as that of the sale and consumption of bread or gasoline. This means that what is desired is a war which will never end, which will survive and which cannot be killed. No wonder that those of our fellow men who criticize and try to subvert this situation are called and treated as subversives.

According to the basic lie of our epoch, the production of weapons is needed in order to prevent wars. The truth is, on the contrary, that wars are needed in order not to prevent the production of weapons. It is for this reason, in order to guarantee the production of weapons, that wars are being produced. Thus, they are a means of production.

Nothing is more dishonest than cowardice cloaked as justice or as fairness. Many who fear to be slandered or to be called "biased", have made it their scandalous principle never to mention an aggressor belonging to the so-called "Free World" without simultaneously discrediting his victim, too. Whoever says something against a President Nixon pretends to be morally obliged immediately to add something against a Chou En-lai, and thereby to prove how objective and how just he is. In a way this cowardly tactic amounts to acting as if we believed in the existence of a universal "equilibrium of guilt" or a "balance of infamies" – a simply ludicrous belief which would imply, for instance, that as many American women and children are being slaughtered by Vietnamese napalm bombs as Vietnamese women and children are being slaughtered by American napalm bombs. And this is not only nonsense but outright hypocrisy and fraud. I am afraid that this fraud in our European and American peace movements will eventually cause their moral ruin. He who applies the same yardstick to the murderers and to the victims is taking sides: for by accusing both of the same violence, he is excusing the aggressors. Let's leave this task to the murderers themselves.

If we confine ourselves – and this danger exists in the anti-atomic movement – to fighting against nuclear weapons, we prove that we have not mastered the ABC of our epoch. There are those who believe that the B and C (the bacteriological and chemical) weapons or the new mechanical gadgets, such as the "lazy dog", which are being "tested" and developed in Vietnam today, will not provoke the final catastrophe of mankind, at least not as directly as the atomic weapons, and that, for this reason, they are less dangerous. This argument leads to a frightful self-delusion. If these new weapons are so often belittled as being "only comparatively dangerous" or "only conventional," or if they are even being welcomed as "human," this has become possible only because today's blackmail of total nuclear destruction has become the yardstick with which the magnitude of other weapons is being measured. In other words: the production and the daily testing and usage of the new weapons in Vietnam are taking place under the protection of atomic blackmail. This is indeed a "shield" – though not in the sense in which the manufacturers and managers of public opinion like to use this word today. For it is not peace or mankind which is being shielded by the nuclear deterrent, but rather the production of those means of destruction the effect of which is not total; and it is not only the atomic weapons themselves which we have to fight but just as energetically the production of other types of arms.

On July 3, 1966, two American jets tried to support some units of the US 1st Infantry Division which were engaged in battle with the Viet Cong. However, the napalm bombs missed their mark and fell upon the American soldiers twenty of whom, screaming, their clothes ablaze, died in the mud. What should we say? Should we perhaps exclaim: "How ghastly that such accidents are possible!" Wouldn't this imply that it might have been less frightful – even not frightful at all – if the American pilots had aimed more precisely so that only Vietnamese would have burned to death? This would be infamous. However, it would be no less infamous to welcome this "mishap" and to stress that at last the aggressors now had the chance to experience what they are doing to others. And no less infamous to say: "Now maybe they will learn that this misfortune was not an exception; that they are always hitting themselves, even when they believe they have hit the mark and have struck only the enemy." These arguments, however true they may be, are no less vulgar than the words of those who regret that the wrong people were burned to death. After all, these American soldiers are victims too; even those who may enjoy their bloody work and who may be proud of it, since others drilled them to enjoy this sort of pleasure and this sort of pride. Even worse than the other responses was that which General DePuy of the 1st Infantry Division made after this terrible misfortune had struck his unit. In a tone which he meant to sound dauntless, but which, in reality, only betrayed his utter emotional illiteracy, he stated: "We are not angry at the Air Force." In order to stress the harmlessness of this "mishap," he commented that, after all, "this was an error of only about 50 meters." Apparently General DePuy felt and wished to convey that the accident would actually have been appalling if the bombs would have missed their mark by 100 meters – that to err is human, human even when through an error B goes up in flames instead of A; that, after all, in the game played in Vietnam such human errors cannot be excluded; that it would be inhuman to expect that every bomb could hit its target; that it would be unfair to demand such inhuman achievements, even in the war against the Viet Cong. In his words, which are obscene, although he may have meant them as words of consolation: "It's the chances of the game." Game indeed.

As an ingenuous gesture – "we have nothing to hide" – the Americans have repeatedly not only admitted but even emphasized that they have accidentally bombed wrong villages in Vietnam. Nothing is more deceitful than such an exhibition of veracity. For by stressing their error in having bombed this or that village, they are implying that their bombing of other Vietnamese villages has been and will be legitimate. Whenever a criminal volunteers a confession, we have to ask which untrue supposition he thereby tries to make us believe to be valid.

Those – and amongst them are even chancellors and presidents – who like to compare the number of war deaths with the number of traffic deaths, and who then triumphantly proclaim that the number of victims on the highway in the United States is greater than the number of American boys who have fallen in Vietnam, are simply frauds.

Even if their figures should be correct – what do they prove? After all, the number of sex murders is also smaller than that of traffic deaths, but does this say anything in favour of sex murders? Those who make use of such comparisons have no other aim but to lead us to the false conclusion that if we demand the abolition of napalm or lazy dogs (not to speak of atom bombs) we should – or rather, we are even obliged to – demand the abolition of our cars as well. Secretly speculating on our fear of expropriation, they seem to ask us: "And what would you say if we would ask you to give up your cars?"

Unfortunately, it cannot be denied that time and again this pseudo-argument has been successful. When hearing this comparison, most people seem to forget the simple fact that napalm and lazy dogs (not to speak of atom bombs) are manufactured for no other purpose than to kill people – while cars, so I am told, are being produced to transport people, although occasionally they may happen to lead to fatal accidents. And even if it were true (and presumably it is) that there are criminal car producers who, by methodically planning obsolescence of their products, are indirectly planning and committing murder – why should this fact excuse those who are planning and committing murder directly through their production of deadly weapons and genocidal wars?

Of course, it is true – and again and again we must point to the fact – that the Americans are using weapons and gadgets (such as napalm bombs and the lazy dogs) which are banned by international law, and that they are destroying temples, hospitals and schools. And yet, as long as we confine ourselves to protesting against these crimes, we create the utterly false and misleading impression that we wouldn't object to the American aggression in Vietnam if, instead of napalm, only "conventional weapons" were used; if, instead of temples and churches, only "conventional buildings" were destroyed; if, instead of the sick and children, only "conventional people" were liquidated. Under no circumstances should we allow or make ourselves guilty of causing such a misunderstanding. Once and for all we have to state: the real crime is not that the American government is waging its aggressive war with *this* weapon instead of *that* weapon, but that it is waging an aggressive war; and not that it is destroying *this* type of house instead of *that* type of house, but that it is destroying houses; and not that it is liquidating this human being instead of *that* human being, but that it is liquidating *human beings*. What counts is the attack as such. The atrocities to which one commonly points are only crimes of a second degree. *Only crimes within a crime.*

* * *

On July 22, 1966 *The New York Times* published, without comment, a report about the launching of a Polaris submarine, the *Will Rogers*, in Groton, Connecticut ... and its christening by Mrs. Hubert Humphrey. Despite its brevity, this item contains five disgusting, even obscene, elements.

It is obscene

that a vessel, the underwater rockets of which are supposed to commit genocide, was given a name just as if it were any ordinary banana boat or passenger ship;

that this act of naming an instrument of genocide was called "christening";

that no more suitable name could be found than that of a humorist;

that this act of "christening" an instrument of genocide with the name of a humorist was imposed upon a woman; and finally

that this woman – no less than the wife of the Vice-President – apparently carried out this request without any inhibitions.

As far as we are concerned, we can only hope that those millions who may be killed by this instrument will feel consoled by the knowledge that it is not to a tragedian, but to a comedian, and not to a missile "christened" by a man, but to one "christened" by a woman, that they have fallen victim.

* * *

*... We would lose face if we once again stopped bombing North Vietnam
... Official Cliché*

I cannot remember that anyone really possessing a real face has ever argued that, because he "couldn't afford to lose his face," he was forced to undertake this or that – generally something very bloody – or that he, unfortunately, couldn't get out of this or that – generally very bloody undertaking. Whoever possesses a face can rest assured that it will stick to him, that he won't lose it, either in his own eyes or in those of others; it is much easier to lose his hands or his feet. The figure of speech is used exclusively by those who are not only faceless, but so egocentric that it doesn't enter their minds to try to visualise what (if at all) they look like in the eyes of others. If they did, they would, to their never-ending amazement, have to recognise that it has never occurred to anyone to acknowledge as faces those amorphous spots that they themselves, when looking into the mirror, never tire to admire; and that, therefore, all of their bloody efforts, which supposedly serve the purpose of face-saving, are nothing but a waste of time.

No matter whether they ever had a face which they could lose, what counts are the following questions and answers:

1. Whose eyes are murderers thinking of when they fear losing face in the eyes of others by not continuing their bloody work?

Answer: Only the eyes of other murderers.

2. What do they imply and impute by issuing their declaration officially and publicly?

Answer: They imply and impute that by renouncing their bloody job they would lose face in the eyes of everybody; thus in our eyes too – thus that their way of death is our way of life.

3. Are they entitled to thus disgrace us?

Answer: This question can be answered only by our actions.

* * *

News item from Saigon: *During the last week in October US bombers mistakenly attacked the South Vietnamese village of Du Due thereby killing forty-eight civilians and wounding fifty-five.* (Needless to add that the Americans immediately flew medications to the surviving victims and that representatives of the South Vietnamese government promptly expressed their gratitude for this helpfulness.)

When the director of the Molussian* Mafia, Mr. Fu, saw that his third attempt to blackmail the merchant Bim had failed, he decided to apply measures which were customary in such cases: to do away with the oldest son of this unreasonable man. Of course this action didn't cause any difficulties, and when, on the following morning, the specialist reported to the director about the business dealings completed during the night, he could also, amongst others, relate the decease of young Barn. "What?" screamed Mr. Fu to the surprise of his specialist, "the son of Mr. Barn?" "According to instructions," the specialist replied. "Instructions! Instructions! That's murder! I said Bim, not Barn." Whereupon the employee, remarking that one corpse doesn't exclude another, got up and strolled away.

If and how Mr. Fu has punished his specialist for his negligence is unknown to us. But we do know that he was unable to forget the older Barn, who had been thrown into such grief through an effort of the firm. With the promptness which is known only to the truly virtuous heart, Mr. Fu immediately sent a message of his most profound condolence to the bereaved Mr. Barn, and even let this message be followed by an autographed portrait of himself. It is certainly a consoling testimony to the urbanity of Molussia that the old gentleman Barn, despite his unspeakable pain, showed himself worthy of Mr. Fu's humane gesture, and that he not only expressed his gratitude for the unexpected present, but even gave it a place of honour on the wall of his desolate home.

"For five days now," announced the well-known chief of the Molussian Mafia, Mr. Fu, who temporarily had confined himself to slaughtering only the inhabitants of the Southern part of the city, "for five days now I have most puritanically abstained from shedding blood in the Northern suburbs." And after ten days, he bragged in a similar way, and after fifteen his words were even more boastful. "Truly," he concluded his third proclamation – and the ring of his voice was as ominous as that of all moralists who are about to lose their patience – "truly, if there are still

---

* *The Molussian Catacombs* is a novel by Anders which probes the rise of fascism through a series of exchanges between two men imprisoned beneath the imagined country of Molussia.

people in the Northern part of our city who refuse to trust me and who fail to recognise the unmistakable signs of my peacefulness, I'm warning them for the last time. They will have no right to complain about the consequences of their stubbornness."

And not only did his Mafia Brethren applaud, but also the Most Honorable Gentlemen: the members of the city council, since they too despised nothing more than violence and loved nothing more dearly than peace.

* * *

"Join with people!" runs the second commandment. "Understand their life, use phrases from their language, honour their customs and laws!" And the third commandment: "Treat women with politeness and respect!" And the ninth: "Reflect honour upon yourself and the USA"

Urbane recommendations for the use of Fulbright students sent to European universities? Nothing of the sort, but rather rules belonging to the official code of behaviour handed out to American G.I.'s stationed in Vietnam.

"Use their language!" Of course it is idiotic to expect from American boys, many of whom are not even able to speak their own language correctly, that they should, immediately upon arriving in Saigon or in jungle villages which they are supposed to destroy, attain linguistic genius and overnight toss off Vietnamese proverbs or local expressions. But how harmless is this idiocy compared to the hypocrisy on which the other commandments are based!

How should boys who are being sent over in order to violate the population; who are told to poison rice fields; who are encouraged to pose as brothel masters of cities; who, working as torture specialists, are tape-recording the screams of the interrogated and (long live Social Psychology!) "evaluating" these tapes – how should these poor boys carry out such tasks "with politeness and respect?" And in a way which "reflects honour upon themselves and the United States?"

Some months ago in Auschwitz I walked between the mountains of hair, of eye glasses, of suitcases, of brushes, of artificial limbs; between the mountains of those dead objects which, used to being dead anyway, have survived their murdered owners. I know what the Nazis perpetrated in Auschwitz, but I fear that, compared to those American hypocrites, who have formulated and handed out the Vietnam maxims, these Nazis were – horrible to say – men of honour. Never did I hear that employees in the concentration camps were being told to handle their victims with kid gloves or treat them with respect. Never that any SS man or anyone else working in a crematorium was ordered to gain the confidence of those to be liquidated by using their native language, never that anyone had to lure the Jews into the gas chambers in Yiddish. Not that. However dreadfully the word "love your enemies" has been destroyed in Auschwitz, even more dreadful are those who, although ordering or executing the bloody handiwork, dare to pretend to fulfil this gospel commandment and are even impudent enough to offer themselves as its missionaries.

"Chernobyl is everywhere"

Ten Theses on Chernobyl (1986) – Günther Anders

Thesis 4

To distinguish between the military use and the peaceful use of nuclear energy is senseless and deceitful. For we know that the allegedly peaceful nuclear power plants have for some time now, consistently and without respite, threatened not only certain people, or even all of humanity, but have also posed a threat to all life on earth. Their construction and operation are worse than the military use of atomic energy: they participate in a "Herostratic" project. Today, after Chernobyl, now that no one can feign ignorance, their defenders have deliberately committed a crime. This crime is not only called "genocide" – I often use the adverb, "only"! but "globicide", the destruction of the terraqueous globe. The supporters of nuclear energy, and above all the supporters of waste treatment facilities and super-reactors, are no better than President Truman, who ordered the bombing of Hiroshima. They are even worse than him, because today people know much more than that simple-minded President ever could have known in his time. They know what they are doing; he did not. That we, human beings, should die, whether from a nuclear missile or from a supposedly peaceful nuclear power plant, amounts to exactly the same thing. Both are equally deadly. Killing is killing. Dead means dead. Those who are supporters of the missile and those who are supporters of the power plant, those who minimize the effects of the one and those who minimize the effects of the other, are both cut from the same cloth.

The Good Friday Agreement – 25 years on

Helen Jackson

Helen Jackson was Labour MP for Sheffield Hillsborough for 13 years from 1992. During the pivotal period from 1997, she was Parliamentary Private Secretary to three successive Secretaries of State for Northern Ireland. She is the author of People's Republic of South Yorkshire *(Spokesman Books, revised edition 2023, £12.99).*

In March 2023, 50 people young and older gathered in the Central United Reformed Church in Sheffield to discuss the possibility of the different political parties in Northern Ireland coming together again to restore the power sharing institutions. Under the auspices of Labour for Irish Unity, we listened to Geoff Bell discuss his recent book, *The Twilight of Unionism*. Francie Molloy, the Sinn Fein MP for Mid Ulster, and I talked about our varied experiences before, during and since the Good Friday Agreement (GFA) was signed in Belfast 25 years ago.

My focus was around the role played by women in the run up to the Agreement and its fragile and somewhat tortured implementation since. How can women help solve the present impasse created by the refusal of the Democratic Unionist Party (DUP) to take part in the devolved institutions set up under the Agreement?

The Sheffield meeting took me back to my work as Parliamentary Private Secretary to Mo Mowlam. Mo called me the day after the 1997 General Election when Tony Blair appointed her as Secretary of State for Northern Ireland. She said she was off to meet shoppers in the Saturday market in Belfast, so they would understand how she wanted to work with the people to bring about a respite from violence.

When I met her the next day in London, she explained that she wanted me to do the normal Parliamentary work, but also to go over to Northern Ireland as much as possible:

'We can't do this, Helen, without the support of the women! There are only

men running the existing unionist or nationalist parties over there, but it is women whose lives and families are being ruined by the terror, so we have to harness their support.'

My role was agreed with John Chilcot, her senior civil servant, and my Parliamentary life was transformed. Mo suggested I ask Lady Mayhew, wife of the former Secretary of State in John Major's government, to let me have contact details of key women who were helpful. At the same time, Mo would slip me invitations from community groups which she couldn't manage to fit in herself.

Women in Northern Ireland knew that a women's political party that represented communities across the cultural divide was urgently needed. As the deadline for registering a new political party drew near, urgency was required and the Northern Ireland Women's Coalition (NIWC) was formed only just in time. Many remarkable women, leaders in their communities, shared in this achievement.

Monica McWilliams from a nationalist community and Pearl Sagar from a loyalist area become the two NIWC members at the peace talks, which were now underway. At first the women were subjected to considerable barracking from Unionists. Mo asked me to sit in the front row of the visitors' gallery so that the men were aware that Mo would know who to blame for any difficulties. George Mitchell, from the United States, now chaired the 'Talks' process, bringing his excellent negotiating skills to the table and, in due course, the women were listened to carefully. Hillary and Bill Clinton kept in close touch.

Meanwhile, the Peace Process was getting good support from the European Union, which offered a generous 'Peace and Reconciliation' package of funding. This included finance for community based political education and training for the many voluntary and peace groups that were being created.

The final few days of the talks were dramatic, for many reasons. Everyone felt tired and tense. The Unionists were split. Jeffrey Donaldson, from the Ulster Unionist team, walked out to join the DUP led by Ian Paisley, who were against the Agreement. David Trimble and most of his Ulster Unionists accepted it. Speaking afterwards with Mo, she was both exhausted and anxious as she spelt out how she needed the two referendums in Ireland, North and South, to take place before July 12th, the start of the marching season. The necessary legislation had yet to be drafted, agreed with the Irish government and put through the Westminster Parliament. In the North, the Vote 'No' campaign was in full swing whereas the Vote 'Yes' campaign was in its infancy. Women are absolutely crucial to the outcome, insisted Mo Mowlam, so the work intensified between Easter and May 22nd 1998.

Only after a positive vote both North and South of the border could a devolved administration based in Stormont take on the task of power sharing. There was real rejoicing and relief as the YES votes piled up on both sides. Stormont became alive. Mo organised a big party in the grounds, with music from Elton John. David Trimble was sworn in as first minister and Seamus Mallon of the Social Democratic and Labour Party (SDLP) as deputy, working together to bring about peace, reform and stability across the two communities.

Revisiting this remarkable history reminded me that the problems initiated with the Brexit vote are not yet over. Rishi Sunak and the EU's Windsor Framework is a start. It's now crucial to revive a working cross-party devolved administration so that all the population feel empowered to manage their future. We have heard from so many of the participants, journalists and politicians who were at the talks stressing how the Good Friday Agreement model had become an international blueprint used across nations, but only a few have given space or emphasis to the deliberate inclusion of women in the communities to its success. Avila Kilmurray, remains a respected community development organiser across Northern Ireland and told me days before the Sheffield meeting that it is clearly women who want its re-establishment the most. During the questions and answers, all were adamant that no one wants to go back and reinstate a hard border.

Who knows? Another border poll in the future – North and South – peaceful and constructive, might conclude that a united Ireland within the European Union is the best pragmatic outcome for this centuries-old problem.

Adult Education and Workers' Control

Tony Simpson

The recent 'Knowledge is Power' exhibition celebrated the centenary of Nottingham University's Adult Education Department. In the wake of the First World War, the Ministry of Reconstruction established a special committee which, in its final report in 1919, argued that adult education was a 'permanent national necessity'. Such classes fostered active democracy, enriched communities, and nourished curiosity and love of learning. So it was that Nottingham University pioneered education for working class adults. In 1920, the first Department of Adult Education in Britain was established in Nottingham. In 1922, Robert Peers became Britain's first Professor of Adult Education. This story was recounted in some detail in an informative exhibition and a stimulating and well-attended series of public lectures and film screenings. Many former students remember positively their encounter with adult education.

'Class, Community and Adult Education' was the exhibition's sub-title. This echoes the triplet 'Poverty, Deprivation and Morale in a Nottingham Community', sub-title of the landmark enquiry into poverty amongst the working people of the city's St Ann's district. Students from the Shakespeare Street Adult Education Centre surveyed St Ann's residents, calling at their houses. The preliminary findings of the St Ann's Study Group we're written up by Ken Coates, tutor in sociology in the Department of Adult Education, and Richard Silburn, lecturer in applied social science at Nottingham University. Subsequently, Coates and Silburn authored *Poverty: The Forgotten Englishmen*, the classic text familiar to generations of sociology students, which recounts the lives of the working poor and their neighbours. It resonates still.

John Holford, Robert Peers Chair of Adult Education at the University of Nottingham, combined with Manuscripts and Special Collections at the University to assemble a thoughtful and provocative show which posed a question in the mind of this former student why this enriching, creative and mutually instructive practice of adult education has been run down and squandered in recent decades.

In autumn 1979, I enrolled for my first evening class at the Adult Education Centre in Shakespeare Street in the middle of Nottingham. It was 'Political Power in Britain', taught by Ken Coates. I had recently read *Poverty: The Forgotten Englishman*, which I found in a bookshop in Belgrade, where I was researching the Yugoslav 'self-managed' economy. I'd learned some Serbo-Croat in the Department of Slavonic Studies at Nottingham University, which I was applying in studies at Oxford.

Earlier in 1979, Mrs Thatcher had been elected for the first time, and this was to bring many deleterious changes, including for adult education. 'Thatcherism' was just getting into its stride. Ken's vocation was to 'teach, not preach' and it was notable how constructively he engaged with the wide range of political opinions expressed by dozens of adults on a weekly basis. All through the long winter, we turned up because the discussion was interesting and our curiosity was aroused. So it was that horizons broadened, even as 'monetarism' took hold and VAT soared from 8 to 15 per cent, while Mrs Thatcher made initial steps to put publicly owned industries, which represented massive public investment in the utilities and other public infrastructure, in private hands. Tony Benn MP was an outspoken critic of her policies.

Benn came to Nottingham to speak at conferences organised by the Institute for Workers' Control. The IWC was formed in 1968, but its Nottingham roots went deeper. In April 1964, a day school on industrial democracy was convened at the Shakespeare Street Adult Education Centre. 'After resting dormant for two generations, the movement for workers' control in Britain has once again begun to stir,' wrote Ken Coates in his 1965 essay 'Democracy and Workers' Control'. That lengthy hibernation stretched back before the First World War and the syndicalist upheavals nurtured by Tom Mann and others. Coates shared an interest in and enthusiasm for syndicalism with Bertrand Russell, with whom he was starting to work. Coates recalled that the Shakespeare Street meeting attracted more than a hundred participants 'drawn from most unions and a number of universities' (*Workers' Control: Another world is possible,*

Arguments from the Institute for Workers' Control by Ken Coates, note 3, page 54).

The Nottingham meeting highlighted the participation of adult educators from elsewhere in Britain such as Michael Barratt Brown from Sheffield and founding principal of Northern College near Barnsley, and Tony Topham from Hull University. Topham was central to the success of the Nottingham meeting in attracting wide participation. This network of adult educators also included John Hughes, warden of Ruskin College, Oxford. Audrey Wise MP was to chair the IWC. Its secretary was Ken Fleet, chartered accountant and participant in the St Ann's Study Group.

Adult education and the Labour Movement's engagement with industrial democracy again became closely connected. Tutors learned from their students, as many have publicly acknowledged, in two-way exchanges. This process is extensively documented in the archives of the IWC and of Ken Coates, held at Nottingham University's Manuscripts and Special Collections, which assembled this important and timely exhibition.

Adult education remains a 'permanent necessity' in the 21st Century, all the more so as the need currently goes largely unmet.

THE
Week

A NEWS ANALYSIS FOR SOCIALISTS   VOL. 2. No. 4. 30th JULY 1964   **9d**

Workers' Control and Socialist Strategy

Tony Topham

In 1962, Tony Topham joined the adult education department of Hull University as staff tutor in industrial studies. In April 1964, with Ken Coates and others, he actively organised the first conference on workers' control to be held in Britain in many years, which met at the Shakespeare Street Adult Education Centre in Nottingham. Tony Topham conveyed his excitement at these developments in this short article, which anticipated the election of a Labour Government after 13 years of Tory rule. Tony's article is based on the postscript to a longer piece which he wrote for New Left Review *entitled 'Shop Stewards and Workers Control'. The present article appeared in a 'Special Workers' Control Issue' of* The Week, *a news analysis for socialists which commenced publication in Nottingham in January 1964.*

The Conference, convened by *Voice of the Unions* at Nottingham on 25th-26th April [1964], was the most representative of its kind on the issue of Workers' Control since the 1920s, and the developments that will inevitably flow from it have placed this question firmly at the centre of socialist strategy for the immediate future. The meeting represented many strands within the left of the trade union and labour movement, included the editors of seven socialist journals, and contained all the major industrial regions amongst the participants. In addition many shop stewards from the East Midlands area attended one or other of the several meetings which comprised the weekend. Altogether some 100-120 people participated. It is certain that *no other single issue* of socialism could have produced such a response to an *ad hoc* and basically spontaneous conference. The echoes will circulate within the movement in the next few months, and in many practical ways, the 'follow-up' activities planned will focus attention on the concrete and immediate nature of the question of control.

The following notes must be regarded as a purely preliminary assessment of the conference and not as a mature judgement. The spirit of the new movement which was created at Nottingham must at this stage be: 'Let a hundred blossoms bloom' through we must work speedily to harden an agreed series of concrete demands.

(1) To deal with certain negative and 'eliminating' tendencies first. There were, perhaps inevitably, references to the failure of various experiments in industrial democracy – for example, the industrial co-operative co-partnerships – in this and other European countries. The conference as a whole was not disposed to take this evidence as requiring a pessimistic conclusion about the current movement, but rather drew the moral that isolated experiments, conducted very often by individual philanthropists with inadequate technical and economic resources, and often in complete isolation from the organised labour movement, and regardless of the objective historical situation, do not provide a reliable guide for a basically political working class movement.

We were also confronted with pessimistic references to sociological findings on workers' attitudes to control, but most people regarded such findings as lacking in any historical sense. It is true that *conscious* articulation amongst workers of a demand for control is limited to a minority, but the situation is changing rapidly. Had similar 'questionnaire-type' research been carried out in the 1910-1920 period in engineering, the results would have been very different, whilst an enquiry in, say, the 1860s, would have produced a different answer again.

Most people at the conference displayed a considerable impatience with the static analysis of sociology, whilst some wished to exclude theoretical discussion altogether, in favour of tackling the immediate need to produce a working class programme. This was for the most part a healthy sign, but the present writer thinks it is absolutely necessary for a socialist analysis and theorising to take place alongside and indeed within the political movement, otherwise we shall have no understanding of the direction in which we want to move. To assume a dichotomy between theory and action is an old historical weakness of the British labour movement.

Thus it was important to have Tom Bottomore's lecture on 'Elites or

Equality' in his particular conclusion that the full development of self-management on an egalitarian basis was only possible after the issue of ownership had been settled: ie, on the basis of social ownership.

(2) To turn to the key issues and areas of concern. There was unanimous agreement on the need to press with utmost vigour for the democratisation of the existing nationalised industries. This general position was developed in one of the working groups which, in its report back, urged the need for legislation to give executive powers to the consultative machinery in the mining industry, as a first step. The Ruskin College Workers' Control Group's draft law for the mining industry, which will shortly be produced for circulation amongst participants, may well carry such demands to further lengths.

Related to the demands for nationalised industries was a well-argued proposal (in a paper submitted by Richard Fletcher) for the transformation of the retail co-operatives into worker-governed, rather than consumer-governed, enterprises. This is a scheme which will certainly receive close attention from the membership of USDAW in the near future.

(3) In the private sector of industry, it was clearly the consensus of opinion that the relationship between the issue of control and the position of the shop steward is a crucial one. The need here was to strengthen the position of the steward, and of his implicit demands for control by searching out issues which he could expect to engage the support of various potential 'allies' – the political labour movement, the white collar employees, trade union officials, etc. by stressing the democratic and liberating nature of many of the shop stewards' demands, his isolation would be prevented, and a movement built on his role. The conference was too short and there were too many preliminary problems of definition and understanding for an agreed set of specific demands for encroaching control to be formulated, though there were many references to such things as the right to hire and fire, the right to determine speed of work, the right to control expenditure, and policy in welfare and safety matters, etc.

(4) On one issue, however – the classic demand for opening the books – the conference was involved in an important debate on the relationship between incomes policy and workers' control. There is an obvious need for a positive attitude on the part of advocates of workers' control towards the economic policies of a future Labour Government: the issue concerns our whole basic strategy. To understand this, it is worth quoting the perceptive comments of an Italian socialist on the British scene. (Antonio Lettieri: 'The Trade Unions and the EEC', in *International Socialist Journal,* No. 1):

'The three conflicting theses at the 1963 TUC Congress on incomes policy seem to provide a good example:

(a) The thesis of Woodcock, which favoured regulating wage demands in the context of planning concerted with the leaders of the industry and with the Government – which corresponds in substance to the thesis of integrating the trade unions into the system with a rationalising function and which, if it was rigorously put into practice, would lead to a withering away of the unions' autonomy:

(b) the thesis of Ted Hill, opposed to any wage control in the present situation – a thesis which was approved by the majority of delegates thanks to the dedication and support of Cousins:

(c) lastly the thesis of Cousins (which emerged with that of Ted Hill in the voting, but was substantially different), which affirmed the possibility of accepting an incomes policy, but only in certain conditions, viz. under a Labour Government.'

At Nottingham, the 'Cousins thesis' was *developed* and *expanded* to embrace the demand for control, under the slogan: 'NO INCOMES POLICY WITHOUT WORKERS' CONTROL' or alternatively 'NO INCOMES POLICY WITHOUT A WORKERS' VETO'. This poses a fundamental challenge to property income, since it was envisaged that workers' control or the veto would apply to the distribution of profits … However, the slogan raised fears in the minds of some speakers who could be said to defend the 'Ted Hill thesis'. They argued that the endorsement of an incomes policy involves a condonation of the system of private profit, which it was the business of the unions to attack without condition until the transformation of capitalism to socialism was complete. In the light of this debate, Lettieri's comment on the theses is invaluable, and may help clear away misconceptions about the slogan.

'Of the last two theses, that which advocates absolute opposition to an incomes policy, although presented as being the most concerned for the unions' autonomy and the most combative, in fact risks being proved to be ineffective, to the extent that it offers no perspective for the solution of those problems which in recent years have seized the British socio-economic system. The intermediate thesis of Cousins, on the other hand, implicitly introduces into the argument certain interesting qualifications: the unions, he stated in substance, can consider an incomes policy in a different political context from that currently prevailing – with a Labour Government. **If this analysis were to be**

deepened, *it could signify that the trade unions are not prepared to slow down their demands simply in order to let the economic system catch its breath, but are, on the other hand, prepared to fix a correlation between their own actions in support of demands and a line of economic policy **whose aim would be a certain kind of reform of the present structure.**'*
(Loc. cit. : my emphasis) ...

(5) On the organisation level, the conference agreed to pursue the issue of workers' control through local study-groups, through the establishment of a regular clearing house of information, and through a reconvened national conference in the near future. Before the latter can advance the movement fruitfully, we need an extended and intensive debate in print. Can we appeal through these columns for all who have a concern for its advancement to 'get it down on paper'? Letters to the socialist press, articles for journals, can all help this developing process.

ANARCHY 40 TWO SHILLINGS or THIRTY CENTS
The Unions & Workers Control

Unions and Workers' Control

Colin Ward

The writer Colin Ward participated in the weekend meeting about industrial democracy, which was held in Nottingham in April 1964 and we are pleased to reprint with permission his report of the proceedings, which appeared in Anarchy *magazine, now available online (thesparrowsnest.org.uk).*

The study group on industrial democracy held at Nottingham in April (and convened by the journal *Voice of the Unions*), concerned itself largely with the policy and demands to be adopted by the unions if and when a Labour government is returned in the autumn. Ernie Roberts of the AEU [Amalgamated Engineering Union] pointed out that there were many Labour party resolutions on the subject which had never been implemented: 'Cripps said that the workers were neither fit nor ready to control industry. Morrison not only said it, but made certain that it would be so.' Ken Coates reminded the participants that their discussions were taking place in the context of a capitalist system which is moving closer and closer to state capitalism: the direct opposite of workers' control; and several other speakers pointed out that unless the Left built up now a movement for workers' control, the initiative would certainly be taken by the right wing of the Labour Party, to divert left-wing militancy, whether in the nationalised industries or 'co determination', under the banner of 'orderly industrial relations', productivity, and so on.

Participants differed in their assessment of the extent to which a demand for workers' control can be said to exist. Peter Jackson pointed to a recent survey in the steel industry, showing a desire for workers control of 15 per cent. (But think: if only 15 per cent of workers *were* actually and actively demanding workers' control!) Other speakers were sure that a revival of the idea within the trade union movement was imminent, if not already in evidence: Tony Topham, for instance, drew this conclusion from the sharp growth in the number of shop stewards in the engineering industry, and the simultaneous increase in the number of strikes over 'non-economic' issues in the industry. 'The number of disputes concerned with management prerogatives', he declared, 'is growing all the time'. There is evidence the employers realise this, and much of the discussion following the Rookes v. Barnard case has been aimed at disciplining the shop stewards, as have the proposals to run 'educational' courses aimed at indoctrinating them.

Topham has developed this theme in a subsequent article, citing Prof. H. A. Turner's study of the increase in stoppages in the mining industry, which Turner interprets as showing 'an implicit pressure for more democracy and individual rights in industry' since 'it seems clear that ... one is dealing with a strong contemporary current of feeling which has not so far been satisfied by the limited development of joint consultation'.

Richard Fletcher, a London Co-operative Society committee member, who led the discussion on the role of workers' control in the Co-op movement, pointed out one curious aspect of that movement's current malaise. In the recent London Co-operative Society elections, under two per cent of the members voted. It was estimated, he said, 80 per cent of the people who actually voted were co-op employees, ex-employees or relatives of employees, with a result that a kind of accidental *de facto* workers' control exists. How paradoxical, then, was the situation in the Works Department of the London Co-op, where the left-wing militant members of the committee have, at short notice, declared 200 of their staff redundant. Here, surely, was a field for experiments in workers' control under a collective contract or self-management system: to operate the Works Department as a syndicate or workers' co-partnership building, for example, houses for co-op members.

This led to some pessimistic observations from Peter Elderfield, based on his experience of trying to organise and to keep solvent co-operative co-partnership building firms. And yet, as he pointed out, co-operatives have built 750,000 houses in Germany since the war, the French producer co-ops have built 400,000 houses, and in Sweden 40 per cent of all housing was built by co-operatives. (Might not the basis of his unhappy experience be not so much the inability of workers to organise on their own, as the difficulty of operating, with insufficient capital, within the framework of a capitalist economy?)

Everyone seemed agreed that if we are going to develop a movement and a demand for workers' control, it must be within the trade unions, and at the same time it was recognised that the unions were not the appropriate vehicle for workers' control. As Tom Bottomore put it in his address on the second day, two separate systems of organisation are needed, since the trade unions could not manage the plants and represent the workers' interests defensively at the same time.

And Michael Barratt Brown, who led the discussion on the possibilities for action in the publicly-controlled industries, suggesting that the first step for 'encroaching control' in the mining industry was on three kinds of policy decision – safety, hire-and-fire, and manning of the coal-face, remarked that while the NUM should be the channel for workers' intervention in decision-making, 'the delegates should not be the little demi-gods who run some of the union lodges'.

Indeed, once we get this issue of workers' control back on the agenda, the question of the role of the unions and of the shop stewards' movement to the two opposing functions of workers' management and workers' defence, is one of the two basic theoretical issues to be argued about. The other is that of the relationship of the idea of economic planning to that of workers' control, which was the subject of a stimulating paper presented to the study group by Walter Kendall of USDAW [Union of Shop, Distributive and Allied Workers]. Basing himself on the experience of the East European countries he concluded (among other things) that 'total planning and workers' control are incompatible. The precondition for workers' control at the point of production is a form of planning which is flexible, general and democratic. Democratic workers' control of production is incompatible with undemocratic control of planning.'

What productivity?

Regan Scott

In February 2023, the former research director of the Transport and General Workers' Union wrote to the Financial Times, *which didn't publish his letter.*

The UK economic policy carousel seems to have shuddered to a halt with the productivity challenge. My Alma Mater Cambridge appears to be a 'hub' for new thinking (Professor Diane Coyle's Bennett Institute for Public Policy) so I thought some reflections from the 1960s and 70s might help the public narrative. This is because I became the desk productivity person at the then Transport and General Workers' Union (TGWU, now UNITE), a trade union 'first', and have worried at productivity issues ever since.

Firstly, there is no macro manipulation solution to low productivity. The unemployment and lost output (growth) costs are far too high. But history may offer some lessons, and economic realism some different orientations.

My experience of the Wilson years suggests how different our economy is today, for good or ill. Strategically dominant and compulsively re-engineered financial services feeding personal services and retail economy pose big questions about even where to start on the issue of productivity. In contrast, those years — the Wilson era — saw the productivity issue being grasped and honed. In many respects, I think history shows that we did get somewhere, in ideas, policy and practice, and performance.

In economic theory and policy, I remember Jack Jones, my boss and member of 'Neddy' (National Economic Development Council) saying that all the talk was of ICORs (incremental capital output ratios). He was a productivity/high wage advocate. I had to read and distribute the reports of the National Board for Prices and Incomes with their open-ended productivity remits, service the Industrial Training Boards and their levies, do hands-on consultancy for union members, and develop trade union policy.

With the wisdom of experienced negotiators, we developed a policy of productivity sharing by collective bargaining: one third to workers (no redundancies, maybe work pattern/hours changes); one third to the company for investment; and a third for shareholders, accepting that we were pushing for works pension schemes and had their interest in financial investments in mind. For consultancy and to prove it was more than rhetoric, I borrowed a slide rule from a friend, and went off, as an example, to advise both union members and management at the big Courtaulds man-made fibres plant on Humberside: their productivity deal seemed to have worked. Participation and sharing proved useful and progressive. Less amenable companies faced a 50/50 starting position.

Secondly, the literature of the post-World War Two American productivity teams elsewhere in Europe and in the UK bears study.

Thirdly, we need to ask how the UK has got away with such a record for poor productivity for so many years. Maybe the statisticians and economically literate politicians have been relying too much on enforced public sector productivity norms (2% per annum, well above manufacturing), a Treasury device started in the Thatcher period to falsify real sectoral and competitive issues, feeding a misleading picture through the 'commentariat' and to the OECD, G8s and 10s, IMF, etc.

UK financial services as a global hub servicing the mega wealthy may, I suggest, have produced a productivity paradox. As the wealthy classes get more wealthy, they spend more and more on human services, from high (excessive?) quality items reaching through to low level, unseen services. What is the outcome? Crudely, there are more staff at top hotels, not less; more restaurant waiters and washers up; and more baristas. Productivity goes down. Also, there are more imports and re-handled retail and personal services and logistics, longer supply chains, more workers, and productivity flat or downwards. At the lower end of the economic demand spectrum, there is low pay, minimum wage traps for manual workers, not forgetting the young graduates avoiding student loans payback by accepting low wages. This is not a good basis for service sector efficiency.

The big cloud over all this is the lack of UK ownership of productivity potential areas of the economy. Brexit lurks here: for the record, when we — the TGWU — led the change from anti-Rome Treaty trades unionism to pro EU policy, we did it not just for a Social Europe boost. We also understood real economics, not just at head office but also on the shop floor from involvement with internationally owned employment.

I find Narcissus guilty of an insufficiency
Of self-love.
Me, now, I wouldn't trust reflections –
In water, or in blood.
Ah, *dukhi*, angels – when could you,
For just a moment,
Extract the roots and the pale stalks
Of my deaf and dumb 'I' from mad soil.
When could you arrange one
Short date for me with it,
So it might whisper to me
Its desires.
Once I have lightly kissed it,
I will know that I am alive,
I will know that the 'I' inside me
Is asleep in black-earth depths.

Elena Shvarts 1979
translated by Georgina Barker

Cynthia
ODDMENTS
II

My Propertius has returned to me again –
What luck, what joy for Cynthia!
Scratched, mauled, bedraggled,
Balding, dirty, scrawny.
His eyes dart about so pitifully.
Why won't you look me in the eyes?
Surely you aren't ashamed in front of me?
You must be ashamed before someone else – love,
For against our will
She runs after me and you
And to our shame and woe brings us back together again.
Oh, how I would like to throw you out
On your ear – only I feel sorry
For that poor little sister, love,
In a pitiful state, but alive, all the same.
Go and change your toga, this one's all stained,
See to your scratches, get washed,
Then fumigate yourself from the filth with sulphur.
Apparently, such is my fate...

Elena Shvarts *1980s*
translated by Georgina Barker

SPQR in the USSR

Elena Shvarts's Classical Antiquity

Georgina Barker

LEGENDA
Modern Humanities Research Association

Reviews

The Russian Girl

Georgina Barker, *SPQR in the USSR: Elena Shvarts's Classical Antiquity*, LEGENDA, Modern Humanities Research Association 2022, 360 pages, hardback ISBN 9781839540533, £95

At the time of writing (January 2023), I had found no other reviews. Various of Shvarts's poems are read in English and Russian on YouTube, where there is also a discussion of her belief in Scandal as the motivator of History, which reminds one of Oscar Wilde's ' I never talk scandal ... History is Gossip'.

Georgina Barker is the Leverhulme Early-Career Fellow in the Department of Greek at University College, London. Her academic expertise combines Classical and Russian Literature, the ideal combination for this study. Barker had paved the way for this with her 2017 University of Edinburgh dissertation 'Russia's classical alter ego, 1963-2015: classical reception in the poetry of Elena Shvarts, Il'ia Kutik. and Polina Barsova' — a detailed abstract is available at the British Library's EThOS website.

Shvarts had previously been given her due by Josephine von Zitzevtz in *Twentieth-Century Russian Literature* (2002, eds. Katherine Hodgson, Joanne Shelton, Alexandra Smith), which is available online and is unmentioned by Barker. Disclosure: I have no Russian, must rely on translations by Barker and, for example, Sasha Dugdale who wrote Shvarts's obituary in *The Guardian* (6 May 2010, available online). Her translation is entitled *Birdsong on the Seabed*. There is also a bilingual edition of her selected prose and verse entitled *After Paradise* (2020).

I shall be concentrating on content and purpose rather than style. There are many website articles about Shvarts, some of which I shall indicate as they become relevant, especially items not listed in Barker's bibliography.

My title is that of a Kingsley Amis's 1992 novel, a valuable adjunct to the volume here under review. It is about a much-touted Russian poetess, Anna (a nod to Akhmatova?) Danilov, who comes to Britain to be fêted and do a series of readings. Trouble is, everyone (including her sponsors) soon conclude that her poetry is worthless trash. Amis concocts an obscenity-laced example of it. He also offers this perceptive general observation:

'this was one of the things people were likely to do under totalitarianism, using poems to send out private messages as well as ... instead of ... without necessarily...'

SPQR in the USSR comprises six chapters, buttressed by copious and welcome footnotes instead of the regrettably usual end-ones, an Appendix of facing Russian texts and English translations, a ten-page Bibliography, a General Index, and Index of Shvarts's works. It is a pity that there is no list of the numerous black-and-white illustrations (many of the very beautiful author) which stud the pages.

Barker's prose is clear and free of jargon, the literary discussions highly concentrated and meticulously documented, plus some welcome diversions, for instance, a comparison between a Shvarts poem and a Monty Python sketch (p178).

To introduce Shvarts I cannot do better than quote Barker's online trailer to the book:

'Elena Andreevna Shvarts (1948-2010) was intellectual, theatrical, apolitical, Orthodox, a Petersburger, hard-drinking, cat-loving-chain-smoking , rowdy... But, first and foremost she was a poet. In her writing, which constitutes one of the most important oeuvres in 20th-21st century Russian poetry, Shvarts broke conventions, donned personae, and transcended "everyday existence". One way she did this was through engaging with classical literature.'

There are aspects here which make me think Shvarts would have welcomed, perhaps joined, the brave Pussy Riot. Whether these women knew much, if anything, about Shvarts, I cannot say. I e-mailed Barker to ask her opinion on this. She kindly replied, finding the notion of any Pussy Riot knowledge of Shvarts unlikely, whilst confirming that Shvarts would certainly have been anti-Putin.

Relevant to this speculation are Laura Little's 'Becoming an Underground Poet: Elena Shvarts and her Literary Environment of the Late Soviet Era' and Marco Sabatini's 'The Pathos of Holy Foolishness in the Leningrad Underground', both online. Catriona Kelly, *A History of Russian Women's Writing* (1994, pages 411-422, unmentioned by Barker) adds a further dimension:

'Shvarts can be described as the most sexually explicit woman since Marina Tsvetaeva and she also has a powerful laconism similar to Tsvetaeva's.'

Shvarts was an autodidact classicist. A diary entry mentions learning Latin at 14. She translated, albeit playing fast and loose with some details, Roman Emperor Hadrian's famous poetic dying address to his soul. If anyone ever updates D. Johnston's 1876 collection of versions of this piece, Shvarts' effort would merit inclusion.

Slipping in alterations to originals is a feature of her verse. For easy example, as part of her regular concern to 'Russianise' Rome, she adds 'ice' and 'cold' to an Horatian ode about warm breezes and soft air (see chapter five).

As Barker insists, Rome not Greece was her chief focus. True enough, in terms of poetic output and personal love of a city which she was finally able to visit in 2000. And she wrote no poems akin to Akhmatova's 'Death of Sophocles'. However, a fair number of her literary 'Alter Egos', discussed at length in chapter two, are Hellenic in name and detail.

One problem about linking Russia with Rome is that the former played no part in classical antiquity. The history of 'Rus' properly begins in 860 with the creation of the cities of Novgorod and Kiev. We must here include Vladimir of Kiev who in 988 chose Christianity over Islam because the former faith allowed him to drink alcohol, though vodka did not reach Russia until 1430, via a monkish recipe.

A major theme of Shvarts' later poems is comparison between the fall of the Roman and Soviet empires. In one poem, this is taken back to the time when Moscow was hailed as 'The Third Rome', which oddly begins 'Istanbul did not fall, nor did Constantinople' since it did succumb to the Turks in 1453.

Not that Shvarts is the only worker in this field, as amply demonstrated by Anna Frajlich's *The Legacy of Ancient Rome in the Russian Silver Age* (2007), along with Pamela Davison's discussion in *Modern Language Review* 104 (2009), pages 618-619 (online abstract available).

As Barker observes, Shvarts did not use Rome to criticize Soviet communism — indeed, how could she? Barker is right, though, to emphasize that her poetry, the very antithesis to approved Socialist Realism, made its own statement. It is beyond question that her more lurid poems, especially the erotic ones, and 'life style' would not have sat well with censorious and prudish officialdom, and would not have gone down well with the Writers' Union.

Barker pinpoints Stalin as a major enemy of the Classics. Shvarts was only five when he died in 1953. There followed the relative 'liberalism' of Khrushchev, the return of repression under Brezhnev, followed by the Gorbachev *Glasnost* years. Though published in translation overseas,

Shvarts did not appear in Russian print until 1985.

Barker portrays Stalin's 'war' against the Soviet intelligentsia as an anti-classical one. This is actually unfair. Apart from the volumes in his own library (see my discussion in *Spokesman* 151 (2022), pages 98-101), we have Molotov's claim that Stalin had 'an exceptional knowledge of antiquity and mythology'. Barker does not take account of Stalin's praise in *The Short Course* (1938) of Lenin's habit of sprinkling his speeches with classical quotations, a matter fully discussed by Hugh Graham, 'The Significant Role of the Study of Ancient History in the Soviet Union' in *Classical World* 41 (1967), pages 86-97.

Furthermore, an unattributed essay online,' The Arts in Russia under Stalin', put out by the Brookings Institution in 1945, states that, in 1938,

'Stalin made a speech in which he declared that the process of purification had been overdone. A breathing space followed. The old tradition re-acquired respectability; the Classics were once again treated with respect.'

Rome for Shvarts was not simply a vehicle for highlighting parallel imperial declines. It was her primary literary source. In chapters three and five, Barker presents in astounding detail analyses of Shvarts' debts to the Roman poets Propertius and Horace. Propertius was a leading Roman elegiac love-poet operating alongside Horace, Tibullus, and Virgil in the reign of Augustus (27BC-14AD). Another inspiration was the somewhat earlier Catullus, famous for his passionate poems of love and hate, well laced with obscenity.

Shvarts' Propertian enthusiasm comes out in her 'Kinfiia', regarded by Barker as ' undoubtedly one of the great works of Russian literature' (page 96). Kinfiia stands for Cynthia, with whom Propertius was long enamoured. He frequently calls her *docta* (learned) and herself a poet. What Shvarts did was to re-create her lost poems. Barker might here have mentioned the comparable 'Homage to Sextus Propertius' sequence of poems by Ezra Pound.

Chapter five is devoted to Horace, who came to prominence in 18th-century Russia, precisely the time when he was the supreme model for English neo-Latin poets such as Samuel Johnson. Shvarts hails him as 'Musagetes' (Leader of the Muses), using this conceit for both serious and comic purposes. Again, Barker's analysis is meticulously all-embracing, fortified by her background notes to the texts in her Appendix. One shining example of her ever-vigilant eye is spotting a Shvarts poetic debt to Elizabeth Barrett Browning's 'The Dead Pan' (page 205).

Barker has produced a quite magnificent study of one of Russia's most remarkable poets who deserves to be as well known in the West as Akhmatova and Yevtushenko. Indeed, the result may well be one of those very few books which can claim to be the last word on its subject.

Barry Baldwin

Civic Gospel

Andrew Reekes and Stephen Roberts, *George Dawson and his Circle — The Civic Gospel in Victorian Birmingham*, **Merlin Press, 176 pages, paperback, 2021, ISBN9780850367713, £16.99**

When we look at our own times with closure of libraries, the reduction of playing fields, closing down public swimming pools, the assault on the Arts, the Humanities on the run, not to mention the fouling of our waters, we could do worse than follow the example of these Birmingham worthies. They were all men (bar two) and middle class (again bar two and often not from Birmingham). But they approached their religious duty, as they saw it, to improve the lives of those who didn't share their privileges, with great determination and dedication — hence the title 'Civic Gospel'.

George Dawson, though appearing in every chapter, has only one short chapter devoted to him. Of Baptist background, he broke from the Baptists and joined the Unitarians, founding a church which seems to have been more of a working man's and woman's college. He was famous for his sermons/lectures inspiring the others who appear here, the most famous being Joseph Chamberlain (father of Neville). They didn't like the Anglicans and opposed W.E. Forster's Education Bill of 1870 because of its religious clauses. They were strictly non-sectarian but passionate about education. This, of course, raises a mountain of questions about what education is.

Science seems to produce ever nastier weapons and most graduates end up in some way or other working in/for 'defence'. It doesn't seem to produce very happy societies: poverty, inequality, 'lives of quiet desperation' where half the population appears to be on medically prescribed drugs to get through the day and the other half on illegal drugs, and quite a number on both. It is quite justifiable to think education is now about stopping people thinking for themselves and is there for turning out the cogs that keep the infernal, social machine running. Some of these Victorians went along with that. 'Educated' and happy men and women make for better workers. Easy to sneer, but in our gig and short-term contract economy, it doesn't seem such a bad idea to treat workers well. I am sure thousands of workers today wouldn't say 'no' to a patronising, paternalistic boss if they were paid well and treated with respect.

But it sometimes went deeper than that: there was 'the existence of a feeling...that there were greater things than vast mills and machinary'. There

> *'existed the desire... that the only objective to be sought in the education of children should be something higher than the mere attainment of such knowledge as would enable them to become better workmen and gain larger wages (But also)...to raise them to a higher level in which the pleasures of literature, science and art might be opened out to them.'*

And these good men and two women put their money, time and energy where their mouths were. They founded institutes and colleges and libraries, art galleries and schools, which they insisted should be beautiful, well ventilated places that did honour both to what was being taught and those learning.

> *'One of the highest offices of civilization is to determine how to give access to the masterpieces of art and literature to the whole people.'*

Dickens came to give the inaugural lecture at one such college and noted with approval the high attendance of poor working class people. William Morris was also involved, a true revolutionary if ever there was one. The equality of women and their right to vote was taken for granted. Marie Bethell Beauclerc refined and taught Pitman's shorthand, introduced the typewriter when it was invented, and initiated the first secretarial courses. (Was that enslavement or liberation?)

Today, we witness strikes of just about everybody, growing anger and discontent at the way our supposedly democratic, sophisticated and 'civilised' society is run and organised and can't help wondering how did we lose our way so badly. Over a hundred and fifty years ago one worthy was writing

> *'a bad teacher was dear at any price and to retain a good teacher was the best economy.'*

It's so obvious and applies to all professions (and I include any job worth doing because of its *real* social value as a 'profession') and yet we see thousands of burned out, experienced workers leaving the jobs they love because of the conditions under which they work and how they are paid and treated.

It wasn't all art and beautiful buildings and parks. One of the worthies boasted with every justification,

> 'our streets are well kept, lighted, drained and watched, the private monopolies of gas and water have ceased to exist [while] the health of the community is cared for by an efficient sanitary system.'

So much for modern 'Progress' — who would have thought those stuffy old Victorians had anything to teach us?

Nigel Potter, Honduras

Chagos -- Colonial Legacy

Philippe Sands, *The Last Colony: A Tale of Exile, Justice and Britain's Colonial Legacy*, Weidenfeld & Nicolson, 2022, 224 pages, hardback ISBN 9781474618120, £16.99

The United Nations 'has promoted the principles of sovereignty and self-determination even through the Cold War and its aftermath' claimed then Prime Minister Truss in her speech to the 77th session of the General Assembly in September 2022. The same cannot be said for the United Kingdom, the governments of which have repeatedly broken such principles.

As Philippe Sands demonstrates in *The Last Colony*, one of the starkest examples of this unprincipled behaviour is to be found in what the British government refers to as the British Indian Ocean Territory – or BIOT for short. The victims of Britain's breaches of principle – and those of us who are outraged by such things – know BIOT by the name 'Chagos'. In 1965 the United Kingdom split the Chagos Islands from Mauritius. It did this in direct contravention of United Nations rules, which made clear that the process of decolonisation should not involve splitting or removing territory. The UK acted illegally. The Chagossians demanded the right to self-determination. This right is enshrined in the UN Charter. Britain refused their demand: again, illegally under international law. Instructively, this same right to self-determination was invoked by Britain to legally justify its actions during the Falklands/Malvinas War of 1982. As late as 2015, whilst still denying similar rights to the people of Chagos:

> *[t]he British government would even publish a paper titled* Falkland Islanders' Right to Self-Determination. *It did so with a straight face, as it opposed the right of Mauritius to self-determination in relation to Chagos. One rule for whites, another for Blacks.* [p 69]

Over and over again, Britain ignored the plight of the Chagossians – a people who had been ripped from their land, transported across oceans and left to suffer. Britain inflicted suffering, injustice and worse on the Chagossians in contravention of international law whilst presenting itself as a champion of a 'global rules based order'.

It was not until 2017 that things started to change for the Chagossians, who refused to give up the fight. In June that year, the UN General Assembly voted 94 to 15 to ask the International Court of Justice for an Advisory Opinion on the legality of the initial separation. On 25 February 2019, the ICJ ruled 13-1 that the UK was under obligation to reverse the separation: to give Chagos back. It took until 3 November 2022 for James Cleverly, British Foreign Secretary, to announce the UK's willingness to begin negotiations for a return: but with one condition – the continued operation of the US military base at Diego Garcia.

Diego Garcia is an enormous airstrip for the United States. It is the place from which bombing raids on Iraq and the wider Middle East have been launched. As Sands explained in his earlier books, *Torture Team* and *Lawless World*, Diego Garcia was also used as a torture site. He notes:

> *In 1945, Britain and the United States had committed themselves to a rules-based international order, then they flaunted the rules. They committed themselves to …[a] vision of decolonisation and human rights, then shredded their own commitments.* [p 130]

The Last Colony is not only an indictment of the conduct of the United Kingdom and United States. It also offers something just as important. As with his two previous works – *East West Street* and *The Ratline* – Sands narrates the determined efforts undertaken by remarkable individuals to ensure that such crimes, such horrors and such crass breaches against humanity are never replicated. The efforts narrated in *The Last Colony* would encompass Sands himself. He is not only a gifted writer but also a practising human rights barrister. Of course, Sands does not put himself centre-stage in the story of how the people of Chagos eventually secured some progress in their quest for justice for their decades of mistreatment: he quite rightly lets the people speak for themselves. Madame Elysé, forced off the islands as a girl by the British, is one such person. When, in September 2018, the case of the Chagossians finally made it to court in The Hague:

> *Unscripted, Madame Elysé spoke from the heart, she knew exactly what she wanted to say. The British Solicitor-General, Mr Buckland, seated just a few feet away, barely looked up as she spoke, an unused pencil clutched in his hand. The Foreign Office legal adviser leaned on his left arm, apparently averting his eyes from the screen. The judges adopted postures of their own ... Some listened to the language of Creole with eyes shut, some focused on the screens, some gazed around the room.*
>
> *After Madame Elysé finished there was a long silence, as powerful as the words, then the sound of tears. The judges listened and heard and, after five decades, it was no surprise there should be emotion. The issues before the Court were not theoretical or abstract. It concerns real people, real lives, real facts, real continuing consequences ...* [pp125-126]

We are now more than five decades on from Britain's theft of Chagos, five decades on from the original item in this catalogue of human rights and international law abuses. It took five decades for Britain to be finally brought to justice. It took five decades of determined effort to get to this point. How much longer will others have to wait for a similar portion of justice? When justice is delivered, will it be tainted by such things as the insistence of Britain and – we should assume – the United States that they continue to control Diego Garcia?

Tom Unterrainer

Themerson

Jasia Reichardt editor, *Stefan Themerson*, published by the Themerson Estate, 2023, illustrated, 220 pages, ISBN 9781916247420, £42

Bertrand Russell wrote of a community of termites: 'They are engaged in investigating an example of the species *homo*, which they have found recumbent with a lump of lead in its heart'. These termites occupy *Professor Mmaa's Lecture*, a book by Stefan Themerson, for which Russell

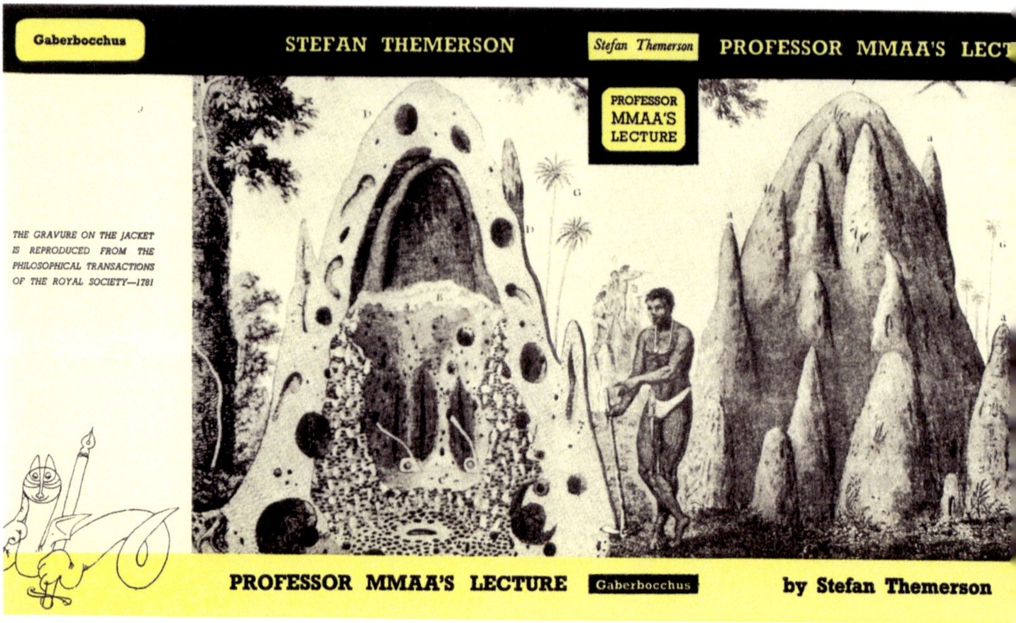

Jacket of *Professor Mmaa's Lecture*

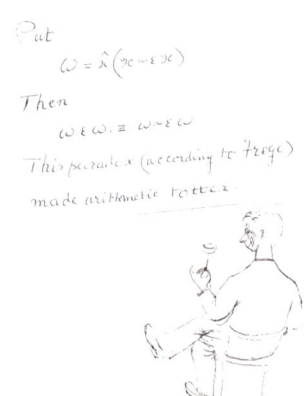

Russell's portrait on the cover of the brochure celebrating his 90th birthday

Russell's equation with Franciszka's drawing

PROFESSOR MMAA'S LECTURE
PREFACE BY BERTRAND RUSSE

I recommend this book to the reader because it is massive, impressive, imaginative, and grimly amusing. I cannot promise the reader that at a point he will shake his sides with laughter, but I can promise him a wr pleasure to be derived from the skilf dissection of folly.

Professor Mmaa's Lecture is a boo belonging to a recognised genre of which the best known example is *Gu liver's Travels*. If I may be permitted the irreverence, I should say that this type of book begins with the account the Germans by Tacitus. The advantage of this type of story used to be th one could invent wise and virtuous beings belonging to some place dista in space and time, like Voltaire's Mor sieur Micromégas or More's Utopian But in our more disillusioned age, we cannot believe in perfectionist drean and our imaginary communities wrote the preface (see opposite). Gaberbocchus (Latinized Jabberwocky) published the book in 1953, with distinctive line drawings by Franciszka Themerson, Stefan's wife and Jasia Reichardt's aunt. Jasia keeps alive the Themerson's extraordinarily creative legacy.

Bertrand and Edith Russell enjoyed a cordial and long lasting relationship with the Themersons. Jasia Reichardt traces its beginning to 1949, when Stefan sent Russell a copy of his collection, *Bayamus*, just then published by Poetry London. Russell replied and a long correspondence ensued, enduring until Edith's death in 1978. Russell had died in 1970. The BRACERS database at the Bertrand Russell Archives, McMaster University in Canada records 321 items of correspondence with the Themersons.

The Themersons, particularly Franciszka, tape recorded Russell recounting anecdotes and stories from long ago, some of which were transcribed and published in *The Collected Stories of Bertrand Russell*, compiled and edited by Barry Feinberg and published by Allen and Unwin in 1972 to mark the centenary of Russell's birth. So it is that we have three Children's Stories, including 'The Post Office of Pinkie Ponk Town'. As Russell explained, 'When my children were very young, we spent the summers a mile from the sea up a steep hill. At the end of a day on the beach, they would find the hill tiring and I tried to take their minds off fatigue by inventing stories …'

Franciszka's delicate line drawings complement Russell's ready wit in *The Good Citizen's Alphabet*, referenced here and first published by Gaberbocchus in 1953, including a signed edition of 100 copies printed on hand made paper. The Themersons had a sure and singular eye for materials, finish and presentation.

This collection from 13 different hands is about much more than the Themersons' relationship with the Russells. Stefan and Franciszka were hugely creative in diverse areas. Nick Wadley remarks of Stefan that 'there cannot be many philosopher-novelists who started their career as visual artists'. It is this visual engagement in photography, film, illustration, typography that brings to life this stunning volume, beautifully designed and printed in The Netherlands, where Gaberbocchus Press latterly found a home. Other Themerson archives are held in Poland. This is a companion volume to Nick Wadley's book about Franciszka, published in 2019 in English and Polish. Thoroughly recommended.

Tony Simpson

Down Wind

Joshua Frank, *Atomic Days: The Untold Story of the Most Toxic Place in America*, Haymarket Books, 2022, 258 pages, paperback ISBN 9781642598285, £14.99

Joshua Frank has written the story of Hanford Nuclear Reservation in Washington State. Hanford was the site of the United States' largest plutonium production facility. Now it is covered with 56 million gallons of radioactive waste. The author claims that the threat of an explosive accident at Hanford is all too real – 'an event that would be more catastrophic than Chernobyl'. It is the most expensive environmental clean-up the world has ever seen, with a $677 billion price tag that keeps growing. Huge underground tanks, well past their life expectancy and full of radioactive gunk, leak, contaminating groundwater supplies and threatening the Columbia River.

Frank goes right back to the beginning of the nuclear story. He points out that this was the land of the of native Americans, the ancestral home of the Cayuse, Umatilla, Walla Walla, Yakama, Nez Perce and Palouse peoples who cared for the land. The book is dedicated to them in their struggles. As the author says, 'we pay our respects to their elders, past and present, and acknowledge that we have benefited from, and continue to benefit from, the ongoing theft of their lands and erasure of their cultures, voices and lives.'

And if you ever doubted how we abused these indigenous people in our greed for uranium (still the fuel needed for nuclear new build), then read Frank's chapter on the horrors of uranium mining. The author shows how people, believing they were doing their patriotic duty by coming to work at Hanford, were actually made sick by working with plutonium.

In an almost unbelievable story, we learn of a man who was involved in a motor vehicle accident while employed as a cement worker at the Manhattan Project construction site. Frank says that the man who was black was a victim of a government that deemed his body was as expendable as his enslaved ancestors. At the Oak Ridge hospital they did not treat his broken bones. Instead, they injected him with 4.7 micrograms of plutonium. The idea, the doctors said, was to let the radiation run through his body. He did not have his bones set until twenty full days after the plutonium infected his blood. The doctor who oversaw this grotesque experiment said the idea was not to kill the man but to see what the injection did to his body over time; to gain a better picture of what exposure to nuclear radiation does to the human body. Even his healthy teeth were yanked out. There was no consent. The man, realising that something was terribly wrong, got up one night and left the hospital. The doctors were apparently dismayed as they had planned to continue monitoring him as the years went on. The man moved away and died of a heart attack nine years after the car accident. As the author says, 'when historians talk about the secret nature of the Manhattan Project, and the scientific ingenuity of splitting an atom to create a nuclear warhead, victims like this man (and there were others) a descendant of slaves in Georgia are rarely mentioned'.

Later in *Atomic Days* Frank discusses nuclear reactors. He points out how nuclear weapons and nuclear energy are inextricably linked. He quotes from Sharon Squassoni, director of the Proliferation Prevention Program at the Center for Strategic and International Studies. 'For the five nuclear weapons states, commercial nuclear power was a spin-off from weapons programs; for later proliferators, the civilian sector has served as a convenient avenue and cover for weapons programs.' In the next chapter, 'Nuclear Plants in the Midst of War', the author states,

'as Russia's invasion of Ukraine demonstrated, the threat of nuclear war is not solely dependent on the detonation of atomic weapons. Nuclear power plants, when located in contested regions or on active battlefields, also pose a grave risk.'

In a further chapter Frank shows how George Monbiot got it wrong with regard to nuclear energy being a carbon-free fuel source. Life cycle analyses find that nuclear power, when every stage is taken into account, actually has a larger footprint than natural gas plant and almost double that of wind energy and significantly more than solar.

Atomic Days is well referenced and I would recommend it to everyone interested in questions of nuclear weapons and nuclear energy. I would also hope it would be read and inwardly digested by all those Tory and Labour politicians and their aides who are supporting nuclear power in the 'energy mix', as they term it.

Rae Street

Who will control renewables?

Dexter Whitfield, *Challenging the Rise of Corporate Power in Renewable Energy*, Spokesman, 2023, 194 pages, paperback ISBN 9780851249186, £18

Dexter Whitfield's new book on corporate power in the renewable energy world is unique in looking ahead and in depth at the implications of high global financial capitalism's penetration of the undoubtedly much needed and welcome renewable energy industries.

Based on his original research of the fast moving financialisation of offshore wind, solar and other renewable energy developments, *Challenging the Rise of Corporate Power in Renewable Energy* poses a big challenge to public policy. Who, after all, will control this vast new global industry? How much wealth will they create, and for whose benefit? These question can be seen as of even greater importance since none of these sectors woud exist without public licensing, public regulation and infrastructure planning consents, and taxpayer subsidies. By definition, they have come about at amazing scale primarily because of public, indeed global human necessity. Should public sponsorship not entail a proportionate public obligation? Might this not be a principled formula for a socialist energy politics to explore? A version of the *juste retour* of classical Christianity still practised, for example, in France for public works undertaken by private capital.

So, Dexter Whitfield has opened a very big door: what sort of returns on capital should be set? What pricing systems should be applied? Should offshoring ownership be allowed free rein? Should foreign ownership of the UK's vast North Sea wind industry not entail binding policy obligations? Or is the future simply a policy of more and faster renewable energy development and no questions asked?

Here, the big politics of fossil fuels suggest an important lesson. Why? Because the huge, historic and powerful fossil fuel industries have been very clever in public debate, and over many years, in hiding behind the façade of a nuclear renaissance. Since no one knowledgeable about new big base load nuclear power reaching 25% to 50% of so-called 'low carbon' energy output really believes it can happen, one has to ask how the gap will be filled and by whom? Guess who? The fossil fuel gas producers. That's real, hard capitalist survival and capture strategy in action. And the public policy response colludes: 'if only renewables could advance faster, but they can't or need too much subsidy,' so, head in hands, for energy security, gas will have to fill the gap. That's the geopolitical game plan that is going on today, and is very evident in the UK and the USA's energy plans.

Might not something similar happen with renewables — a turn from white knight to energy power consolidated into a wealth producing market? Another global profits bonanza outside the control of consumers and governments? Might not the much vaunted global 'green transition' finish up being controlled and owned by the same people and for the same reasons as the historic fossil fuel industries?

What Dexter Whitfield has done is to start a very necessary debate, which might be called the 'double renewables debate' — a DRD alongside PPPs (public-private partnerships) and ESGs (environmental, social and governance). It is time, then, to properly celebrate renewable energy development but, equally, to renew the debate about accountability, public control and universal benefit.

Regan Scott

Simple Twists of Fate

Aleksandar Hemon, *The World and All That It Holds*, Picador 2023, 336 pages, ISBN 9780330513326, £18.99
Ian McEwan, *Lessons*, Jonathan Cape 2022, 486 pages, ISBN 9781787333970, £20

Hemon's and McEwan's audaciously decades-spanning histories take us, respectively, from the assassination of Franz Ferdinand in 1914 to the Shanghai of the 1930s and 40s, and from Suez and the Cuban Missile Crisis to Brexit and lockdown in 2020-21. Their starting-points, in a Sarajevo pharmacy and a Suffolk boarding school based on McEwan's alma mater Woolverstone Hall, are strikingly similar: 'Before he can make any decision, Pinto rises on the tips of his toes, and kisses the Rittmeister right at the border between his moustache and his lips'; 'Her fingers found his inside leg, just at the hem of his grey shorts, and pinched him hard'. Both, it seems, must assert the primacy of the tactile and the sensual, of the propulsive force of desire, before plunging headlong into what Mandelstam and Julian Barnes have called the 'Noise of Time' – transgressive intimacies, but with markedly divergent outcomes. One, the laudanum-enhanced flirtatiousness of a Bosnian Sephardic Jew with an Austrian cavalry officer in search of an aspirin, briefly and preposterously conjures a 'century of progress' for the old empire as a hotbed of sexual and ethnic freedoms, only to find itself swallowed up by the bloody turmoil that erupts a few streets away, the indignities of conscription, the privations and corpse landscapes of war. The other finds McEwan returning almost brazenly to familiar terrain with one of those trademark private instances of atrocity around which whole narratives gravitate (think *Atonement, On Chesil Beach, The Comfort of Strangers*), the incendiary physicality of a piano teacher's grooming and lifelong scarring of her eleven-year-old protégé from which he, and the novel's perspective on the wider epoch, never quite detach themselves.

Hemon has written at length in *My Parents: An Introduction* about their addiction to the Bosnian word *katastrofa*, applied indiscriminately to the potential for misfortune (so as to ward it off, at least psychologically) in almost every situation, 'its particles always shimmering all around us like shrapnel on a sunny day'. *Katastrofa*, though, is insatiable, like the ravening god who presides over the novel – 'The Holy One kept creating worlds and destroying them, creating worlds and destroying them' – and this vigilance counts for nothing in face of the horrors visited on Sarajevo in 1992 that 'crashed into [their] life like a meteorite', or the 'unassuageable longing' for a vanished Yugoslavia that defines the couple's post-war existence in Hamilton, Ontario – just as Pinto's yearning for an idealised, libertine version of his native city accompanies him into the firestorm eighty years earlier. Pinto traverses a geography *ruled* by *katastrofa*, 'a place / Of life and death, / A road / To survival and extinction, / A matter to be pondered carefully' as Sun-Tzu's *Art of War* chillingly announces, the product of a period in Chinese history marked by the same 'absolute insecurity, in which any state might be attacked by a combination of any of the others' (Jenner), 'extreme violence and incessant warfare' (Griffith) displayed again with undiminished ferocity in the 20th century wherever Hemon's incorrigibly random-seeming narrative, as in a lottery, decides to go.

The World begins with a cannon salvo announcing the visit of the Archduke; it ends with a showing of *The Wild Bunch* in a Jerusalem Cinematheque and 'that great shot of a scorpion dropped by a herd of mean children on top of an angry anthill, whereupon the kids watch the poor arachnid being overwhelmed by an army of vicious ants'. Between-times, like a modern day Simplicissimus or Candide (one remembers it was concupiscence got the latter thrown out of that baronial paradise in the first place), Pinto cleaves with the other Bosnian recruits to an image of his own 'safe insignificance … Thank good Allah you are a nothing and a nobody' - and is immediately delivered to the tender mercies, evoked with a visceral, seething lyricism, of the Brusilov Offensive in Galicia (Russians, 500,000–1,000,000 dead, wounded, or captured; Central Powers, 1.5 million casualties; Austrians, 1,000,000–1,500,000); brutally incarcerated in Tashkent amid lice, fever, summary executions; reduced to 'sweat, urine, and faeces ... hunger and despair' in a Makhram hiding-hole in flight from the Bolsheviks; a near-fatality of the massacre by Cossacks and Buddhists of Uighurs at Korla, in the Taklamakan Desert; witness to the pandemonium, 'glutinous terror flowing with the people', of Japan's bombardment of Chapei in 1932; witness, again, to a capsizing Shanghai inundated with refugees and cynical, rapacious Americans in 1949, the Kuomintang in disarray, Communist artillery fire announcing the imminent arrival of the new Chinese masters. 'Nothing good ever happens, Pinto said. But the war will take care of everything ... All the world is, or soon it will become, la gran eskuridad'.

Pinto's is a materialist universe, despite the halo of religious epigrams that derive in large part from his father's nightly recitations of the Torah, and his own Job-like lamentations. It also, courtesy of Hemon's extraordinary mobility through the scenes of carnage – a postmodernist exuberance rivalling the heady freedoms of the early picaresque – bears no small resemblance to the 'monster of energy, without beginning, without end ... force throughout ... a play of forces and waves of force' advocated with devastating prescience in Nietzsche's *Will to Power*. Yet that's only half the story: the essential counterpoint is supplied by the erotic passion that links Pinto to his Muslim comrade-in-arms the mercurial Osman, a 'man [who] never used up the mirth in his oval face, in the flush of his cherub cheeks', and the unending love song this becomes, transcending every situation they encounter, even death. Osman's steadfastness is a more enduring presence than that of any punitive divinity, Pinto discovers, product of '[the] rabbinic chatter in my cursed head', or murderous human agency: 'Osman', he avers, 'you found me at the end of the world, in Shanghai! You were always going to find me, wherever I may have been'.

In *Lessons*, we know where we are. At any point, we feel, McEwan could pull up the drawbridge like his protagonist Roland Baines, and consider child molestation and conjugal separation more than enough *katastrofa* to be going on with: 'A rocking chair, and by it on a low table a book he had bought about world troubles which he knew he would never read. He had troubles of his own. He faced French windows and he was looking down a narrow London garden through a misty wet dawn to a sole bare apple tree'. Europe is first seen, or imagined, as a receding vista reclaiming its own, from which his absconding German wife sends blandly uninformative postcards as she 'drift[s] eastwards, ever further from home … through ten nations and their savage histories'; the globe is a 'boundless' playground for 'mescalin and LSD adventures', from the Rockies to Dalmatia to Kandahar, for a twenty-something Englishman in search of the ecstatic freedoms he'd known as an infant in the army camp at Gurji, evacuated there from Tripoli with his father's unit during the Nasser demonstrations of '56. As the novel proceeds it looks as if history will be a patina of heterogeneous references and half-encounters, 'remote turns in international events' or, as in a visit to Northern Ireland in the '80s, blundering glimpses of a hostile reality that only confirm Roland's innate sense of irrelevance, rootlessness, inconsequentiality: 'In a Knockloughrim pub a fellow in a wheelchair – kneecapped, they decided – advised them to "be careful" … No one touched them, or even threatened to'. Chernobyl instils, briefly, a more destabilising awareness of includedness, Roland retreating behind taped-up windows to largely comic effect – 'He would be a loner and a warrior … He ate from tins and paid attention to the date stamps on the lids' – while entertaining, somewhat anachronistically, the possibility of an even more all-encompassing horror should NATO 'launch a tactical device at Ukraine to halt a Russian tank advance'.

The repeated trips of a young boy 'through the dark, along the muddy tracks' to Miss Cornell's cottage and the 'sensual wonder' he discovers there while offstage, in October 1962, the world is poised to go up in flames, begin ironically to look like the one incontrovertible heroism of a lifetime, except he has a habit of comparing his endeavours to the narrator's in Conrad's *Youth,* avid for imperialism's far-flung adventures: 'Where young Marlowe had his mizzen mast in high seas, Roland had his bike'. But McEwan consistently reserves his bitterest strictures for the post-war or, in 2020, between-wars English generation (his own) as a whole, 'nestling in a little fold of time, eating all the cream', for the liberal intelligentsia chattering at its kitchen tables in the age of Blair and Iraq, for the 'lightweight tales' of a literary orthodoxy '[not] much bothered by poverty, nuclear weapons, the Holocaust or the future of humankind'. He cites instead the activities of the White Rose opposition in the Third Reich, fearless in its calls for European cooperation, 'in the name of intellectual and spiritual values … of intellectual freedom … of moral substance' as its leaflets proclaim, even on the brink of annihilation.

Roland for his part displays a dogged integrity, however ineffectual, in his one protracted attempt to engage with the political situation of the divided Germany, smuggling *Animal Farm*, *The Captive Mind* and other proscribed titles, Dylan and the Velvet Underground masquerading as Shostakovich, into the GDR, and writing letters to Amnesty International when the recipients are arrested. At the East German border, fantasising about the satisfaction he might derive from a night in Hohenschönhausen, the Stasi prison, he stands before a young guard, his own age, who might have stepped straight from the pages of *The World and All That It Holds*:

'The face was pale and long, with a mole on a cheekbone, the lips were thin and delicate. Roland wondered at the chasm, the wall that divided himself and this man who, in another dispensation, could have been a tennis partner, a neighbour, a distant cousin. What lay between them was a vast and invisible network – its interlacing origins mostly forgotten – of invention and belief, military defeats, occupation and historical accident.'

It's all a matter, he thinks later, of a 'Simple Twist of Fate'.

Stephen Winfield

Thanksgiving

I give thanks to You, because in Your mercy You made me a poet,
Because I was born by the Neva and because I am looking at it and
St Isaac's from the hospital window now,
Because Mama and Berta brought me up,
Because I grew up in the shadow of the Theatre,
Because I saw Rome and the globe and Jerusalem,
For the wonderful friends and animals who have accompanied me
(and still do),
For the blessings of inspiration and the joys of pure reason,
For the gift of correct reading of poetry, for my frivolity,
And because You always save me and sometimes I find the strength in
myself to also thank You for the misfortunes.

Elena Shvarts 6 October 2009
(eight days after an operation)
translated by Georgina Barker